Midlife
Myths and
Realities

Other Books by William H. Van Hoose

The Adult in Contemporary Society (with M. Worth)
Counseling Adults: A Developmental Approach (with M. Worth)
Ethical-Legal Issues in Counseling and Psychotherapy
Ethics and Counseling
The Authentic Counselor
Counseling and Guidance in the Twentieth Century (Edited)
Counseling in Elementary Schools
Tecumseh: An Indian Moses (Biography)

Midlife Myths and Realities

William H. Van Hoose

Humanics Limited
Atlanta, Georgia

Library of Congress Cataloging in Publication Data
Van Hoose, William H.
   Midlife myths and realities.
   Bibliography: p.
   1. Middle age.   I. Title.
HQ1059.4.V36   1985   305.2′44   84-25123
ISBN 0-89334-081-2
Printed in the United States of America
Design by Joyce Kachergis Book Design & Production

Humanics Limited
P.O. Box 7447
Atlanta, Georgia 30309
(404) 874-2176

To my son, Fred, and to my daughter, Pam

Contents

Preface

This is a book about *middle age*: men and women in the 40 to 60 age group. The 1980 U.S. Census estimates that more than 60 million people are in this age range. They are the most conspicuous and most powerful group in our society. They are the movers and shakers in business and industry, in government, in education, and in the arts and letters. Middle-aged people control the economy and make the major decisions for all population groups. Yet they are given comparatively little attention in the literature on adult lives.

Much of what is written about this era of the life cycle defines middle age in terms of problems. Midlife people are often described as having problems with their marriage, feeling frustrated with their careers, and being worried about aging and afraid of dying. Terms such as "midlife crisis" and "middle-aged crazy" are so conspicuously and improperly used that many people, including the middle aged, have some serious misconceptions about this stage of life. This leads to unnecessary concern and anxiety.

Many of the so-called problems of middle age have not been properly reported, and several developmental issues of this stage have not been carefully described. This book remedies many of these deficiencies. In the ten chapters that follow, I present adulthood as a distinct stage of life, but a stage that is related to all other stages. The approach is positive developmental: many of the so-called problems are not problems at all, but normal events that occur in most adult lives. Middle age is not a period of stagnation and decline, but a time to keep growing, a time to reach higher levels of productivity and creativity, and a time of greater satisfaction in life.

In preparing this book, I have relied heavily on the available research and literature on this topic, and I have also used data from clients I have counseled over the past five years. Thus, the vignettes and examples are of real people. I have altered some of this case material in order to preserve the anonymity of these people, but I have not altered the reality of their life experiences.

This book is for midlife people who want to understand their own development. But it is not for them alone. People of all ages will find information here that will help them understand others as well as material applicable to their own lives.

Chapter 1

On Becoming Middle Aged

A s Ken and Marianne drove into the town where they had lived twenty years earlier, it at first looked strange and unfamiliar. Then as they entered a residential section and spotted the house where they had spent the first four years of their married life, a sense of recognition came over them. Not much had changed here. Marianne noted that the house looked as though it "has been sleeping peacefully for twenty years." They stopped directly in front of the old house, looking, not speaking, but feeling a sense of closeness to this place—a sense of belonging, but a little sadness as they recalled an earlier life here.

Later, at a midday meal and over a glass of wine, Ken and Marianne recalled the numerous times they had managed a hurried but pleasant lunch in this same cafe. So far they recognized no one, and no one showed signs of remembering them. They shared some memories from this town: the birth of two children, their early financial struggles, and the decision to seek greater opportunities in a large city. They discussed some of the ups and downs in their life since leaving here. Ken wondered what the next twenty years would bring, and Marianne, half-jokingly reminding him that "we *are* growing older," said that she, too, had thought a lot about that lately. Ken, staring into space, wondered what they should do with their lives in the time left to live.

In Ken and Marianne we find a representation of the first stage of a re-examination of life that takes place in many people during middle adulthood. Middle age starts us thinking about what we have done so far and what we should do with our life in the future. In the first three to four years of the period that begins around age 40, a large percentage of both men and women will engage in a rather thorough and often stressful re-examination of all facets of their lives. Careers, marriages, and other human relationships will be reviewed and reconsidered. Future plans and goals will be revised or abandoned; dreams may be forgotten or new ones may emerge. Interests will shift, values will be analyzed, and some commitments will change. This process of review and re-examination is necessary when a person is trying to answer such questions as "Who am I?" and "What shall I do with the rest of my life?"

It is not only the middle aged, of course, who review and restructure their lives. Adults of all ages frequently take stock of the present and make new plans for the future. But we know from several recent studies that there are some unique features of middle age that intensify this re-examination. Daniel Levinson, one of the leading authorities on middle age, believes that society's view of this stage of life adds to the burden of midlife. Our youth-conscious society seems to believe that one is over the hill at 40, and that by 60 one is withered, ancient, and waiting for death. For some this is a terrifying image; they dread middle age, knowing that it is one step away from old age and realizing that this society does not value old people. They cling tenaciously to youth even when signs of aging are readily apparent in the mirror.

During the past few years several psychologists and other behavioral scientists have been trying to learn more about this part of the life span. The work of Levinson, Roger Gould, George Vallant, and others has gained the attention of the academic world and also stimulated popular interest in middle-aged adults. Much of the popular literature on this topic has dealt with middle-aged men and the problems or "crises" they face at around age 40. Men, in the view of some writers, have major problems with their careers and marriages at midlife; women find difficulties with the "empty nest" and menopause. The general message is that at midlife we may fall apart, and that we are entitled to it.

Does this really happen, or is "midlife crisis" merely a catchy journalistic term? Do people really experience a crisis during the middle years, or are we dealing with a myth?

Cultural Influences on the Middle Aged

Our cultural attitude makes us afraid to age, because our culture worships youth. By the time we reach 40 we are aware that we are no longer young. Wrinkle cream, face lift surgery, monkey glands, and "magic" formulas are at best temporary solutions for a growing problem. We are constantly reminded that it is desirable to be young, slim, athletic, and happy. Our obsession with youth is so pervasive that some middle-aged people go to great trouble to maintain an appearance of youthfulness. They get new hairstyles, new hair, new wardrobes, and new partners. Some become depressed and resentful.

The prestige of youth afflicts all middle-aged people to some degree. Men may feel sad and fearful at the first sign of creaking joints and sagging skin, but they rarely panic about aging in the way some women do. Susan Sontag believes that growing older is less wounding for men because society is more accepting of aging in men. According to Sontag there is a double standard for aging that makes the appearance of middle age particularly trying for women. Beauty and sex appeal have traditionally been more important in a woman's life than in a man's, and these features, as defined by our society's youth-worshipping standards, do not stand up well in middle age. Women are valued when they are lithe, young, and feminine; thus their value decreases when they age. No wonder some women lie about their age, while frantically searching for a fountain of youth.

We must also consider the issue of an authentic identity in midlife. Erik Erikson likens identity to a sense of self: a sense of who we are and of our place in society. He speaks of the identity crisis of youth, but acknowledges that questions about identity receive no final answers during adolescence and young adulthood. Identity questions are not resolved when one becomes an adult, but persist into middle age and beyond. For some people, aging heightens the need to deal with identity issues. This is particularly true in the case of persons who dealt improperly with identity questions at an earlier age and whose sense of self has remained blurred or deficient. Now, realizing that time is running out, the middle-aged person is more than ever aware of dissatisfactions with the course of his or her life. Some things do not fit; goals have not been reached, and a unique identity has not been achieved.

Yet, in this century there has been such change in the world, and change continues at such a rapid pace, that identity is harder to achieve. Values change rapidly in a complex society, and it is difficult to judge what is right or wrong, or how to make choices. The estimated 60 million men and women in the 40 to 60 age group in this country in 1980 were born at a time when the winds of change were rising and were thus caught on the first wave of this sweeping change. They were the first to take the giant stride into adulthood without firm ground to stand on. Their footing was washed away by the Great Depression, World War II, and the nuclear age. The old fixed points of reference that existed at the turn of the century have vanished, and they have not been replaced. Everything is open to question, but few questions can be answered. A dedicated craftsman works for thirty years and at middle age finds his work is not valued, his savings eaten up by inflation. A minister discovers that his words have no impact; a TV pitchman has more influence than a Sunday sermon. A patriotic teacher decides that Watergate is only the tip of an iceberg; corruption is rampant throughout the government. These persons have reasons to question their impact on society; they wonder about life's meaning and may have identity problems.

Identity can, of course, survive major conflicts and contradictions, and as we noted earlier, identity struggles are not confined to midlife. But middle age is a time when actions, values, and goals must be harmonized if one is to have a chance to achieve an integrated identity.

Another major societal influence on middle age is the myth about the rewards of middle and later life. Society leads us to believe that if we play our cards right when we are young, we will have a stable and peaceful life when we are older. If we are successful in school, choose the right career, and marry the right person, our future happiness is assured. Society places considerable emphasis upon success, which is synonymous with money, power, and social status. Men, in particular, are expected to show distinction in their careers and make a lot of money before they are 50. The stress caused by this pressure to succeed may be a major cause of heart attacks, ulcers, and other disorders common in middle age.

There is nothing wrong with setting goals and pursuing them with vigor, and I maintain that success is preferable to failure. But if a person's life is bound closely to society's notions about success, middle age may bring disillusionment and disappointment. As I suggested earlier, it can be profoundly unsettling to arrive at middle age and discover that all those things one has worked for have little meaning. Instead of being home safe one discovers that numerous questions remain. Worse, there are no easy answers to questions that continue to arise.

Despite all our attempts to understand ourselves and others we remain quite uncertain about how to live our lives. In this book I explore some of the questions that middle-aged people grapple with as they consider how they should live out their time.

Change and Growth in Adult Life

In his book about adult life, Gould uses the term *transformations* to describe major changes during the life span. *Transition* is another term used frequently in discussing how adults grow and change. Transition also refers to how people move from one stage of life to another and how we adapt to new roles. Nancy Schlossberg defines a transition as an event in life that results in a change of perception and a role change. Naomi Golan writes that adult transitions often result in some personal upheaval, requiring time for re-thinking and adaptation. *Developmental task* is a concept used by some psychologists to describe what people generally do or what they are expected to do at a given stage in life. Freud believed that the major tasks of adulthood centered on *love* and *work*. Vaillant maintains that one can live magnificently in this life if one knows how to love and work. We can also think in terms of *marker events* in studying adults. Some examples of marker events are selecting and entering a career, marriage, becoming a parent, achieving a major goal, getting promoted, divorce, and death of a loved one.

With these definitions as background, we turn to a discussion of some of the major transitions and events in midlife. We have arbitrarily designated 40 to 60 as middle age, but we recognize that middle age is an imprecise method for defining an era of human life. Benjamin Disraeli was accurate when he observed that life is not dated by years; events are sometimes the best calendar.

To live in this world a person must continue to grow and change. During any stage of adult life there is change in various aspects of living: in work, in social roles, and in family and other relationships. Some changes are external, such as in work roles and parenting responsibilities. Other changes can be more accurately described as internal. The passage of time frequently brings a change in perceptions, in values, and in our views about life. Passing years and new events slowly accumulate with the result that we, ourselves, change dramatically and our relationships with significant others and our world in general are profoundly altered. Some of the major changes of midlife as well as the unique features of that period are identified in the following paragraphs.

Some Phases of Midlife

Becoming One's Own Person: Mid Thirties to 40

For men, and more recently for many women, the major task during this period is to become established in a career. These men and women come into their own in the mid and late thirties and break dependent ties with their boss, their spouse, or their mentor. For women whose primary interest has been the home and children, this is a time for greater comfort with the family, but also a period when many begin to pursue independent interests and activities. Some researchers report considerable instability during this phase as people strive for greater freedom and personal satisfaction. Marital relationships that become fragile during the early and middle thirties may become even more strained during this era.

The Midlife Transition: Early Forties

This is the time when a person is likely to ask "Who am I?" and "What should I do with the time left to live?" Some people feel a need to draw up new plans for their lives and in this process, career and marriage come under careful scrutiny.

Entering or re-entering a career often leads to a re-definition of the self, to developing a new image after 40. Annette, age 44, illustrates this point.

A lot of things have happened to me in the last five years. First, going back to school was frightening—no, it was worse—it was almost traumatic. But I knew I had to do something with my life. In twenty years of being wife, mother, cook, and chauffeur, I had lost myself. So I had to find me again. Going back to school did it. By God I discovered I could keep up with the best of them. Soon, they were coming to me for advice, turning to me when they needed help. And I got a job, a good job almost as soon as I graduated. Now I am head of the department. Sometimes that's hard for me to realize. But I don't bring my job home at night, and I think my marriage is better than it has ever been.

The middle-aged person is often trying to achieve some balance between personal interests and the realities of life. There may be several changes in direction as the person realizes that he or she is not going to achieve some goals and that some dreams will not come true. Career changes, divorce, and remarriage are events that occur during the midlife transition, but it remains to be seen whether these are typical or exceptional behaviors in midlife.

Menopause has long been stereotyped as a critical problem for middle-aged women. Now, however, some researchers reject the notion that menopause leads to a crisis in women. Bernice L. Neugarten, for example, believes that the "change of life" is a positive experience for many women. For women whose career was in the home, midlife can be the time to enter or re-enter a career outside the home.

Both men and women must deal with the advancing age and perhaps the death of their parents, the empty nest, the death of friends, and physical changes in their own bodies. These events are clear signals that time is running out. Thus, perhaps for the first time in life, the middle-aged person comes face to face with his or her own mortality. This awareness may trigger emotional reactions that are labeled unstable or "crazy." Middle age, however, does not portend disaster. It may, in fact, herald a new stage of life. Many people do not hit their stride until 40 or later. Erikson maintains that middle age offers numerous new challenges and opportunities, particularly in what he calls "generativity"—nurturing and teaching the next generation.

Settling Down: 45 to Early Fifties

At about 45 a person enters a stable period during which he or she begins to accept earlier decisions and styles of living. The die is cast, and life becomes more settled. New interests and hobbies may develop or old ones may be revived. Money and material possessions become less important. More attention is given to older values and friends. Many married people will re-establish close relationships at this time.

Transition into the Fifties: Early to Mid Fifties

It is still not too late to change a lifestyle after 50. Middle-aged people realize this, and another examination of life and personal goals may be undertaken in the fifties. "It may be late, but I still have time to do my own thing if I start now," is how a 57-year-old man who left a secure job with the federal government to open a hardware store expressed this feeling.

An executive had a similar view:

Frank Worden made it to the top early. By age 52 he had worked for three major corporations and was an executive vice president "with all the benefits." He made good investments and had achieved financial security for his family. But as he put it, "I worked 60 to 70 hours per week and did not often smell the roses." On a long weekend he visited his oldest daughter in Tidewater, Virginia, and according to Frank, those "three days changed my life." He went sailing on Chesapeake Bay, played with his grandchildren, and really "relaxed for the first time in a decade." He pulled up stakes in Connecticut and headed for the Sun Belt. Worden took a job as executive secretary for a professional association at less than 25 percent of his former salary. Both he and his wife are pleased with his new role and with their new life. Part of the fun of the new venture for Frank comes from discoveries about himself. "I have learned a new respect for my fellow man. The people I work for are mainly concerned about serving humanity— not about making money. The satisfaction I used to get from a 'deal' or from the quarterly statements lasted about eight hours. Here the accomplishments are more personal and more pleasurable. And I have some time for living now."

Women may enter an outside career for the first time in their fifties, and like men, women also change careers during the fifth decade of life. People in their fifties report greater feelings of freedom and independence than at any other stage of life.

Stabilization: Mid Fifties to Early Sixties

The significant task during these years is to achieve important goals in the time left to live. Several writers describe these years as a time of mellowing and flowering. There is a softening of feelings, heightened interest in others, a tendency to avoid heated emotional issues, and an increased joy in living.

The stage Erikson calls ego integrity encompasses these years. He believes that if a person accepts the life cycle and is reasonably satisfied with the way he or she has played his or her role in life's drama, the individual will achieve a sense of integrity. However, if one has not come to terms with the major issues of living, disgust and despair may become the dominant sense of this era.

Many of our findings on midlife are tentative. To date much of the research has been conducted on white professional men. Minority groups, women, and working-class men have not yet been the subjects of systematic research.

The data that is available reveals some important differences in the development of men and women, particularly with regard to sex roles and the timing of life stages. Marjorie Lowenthal and her colleagues report some important sex differences in coping styles and in life satisfaction.

While considerably more evidence is needed on this topic, it is nevertheless clear that middle-aged people must grapple with some critical developmental issues. *Biological change, confronting the prospect of our own death, changing social roles,* and questions related to *career and marriage* are all found in the midlife period. The changes that occur during these years are unique to middle age, and the effects of these changes can be explosive and painful. But midlife does not add up to a catastrophe. Unfortunately, when one reads some of the literature on this topic it is easy to conclude that life ends at 40. Midlife is portrayed as a period of decline—the time for backaches and bifocals. Terms such as "middlescence," "midlife crisis," and "middle-age crazy" are now part of our language, even though they convey a stereotyped and inaccurate picture of a majority of middle-aged men and women. Despite some obvious stresses of this period, most people face their problems successfully with strengths developed earlier in life. Thus, the myths about midlife may outweigh the facts available so far. The changes and the pitfalls of this phase are real enough, but many of the reported effects are questionable. In the chapters that follow I hope to shed new light on the middle years of the adult life cycle.

THE DREAM

Much of the midlife re-appraisal revolves around our dreams. Nancy Schlossberg, a counselor and widely respected authority on adult development, writes that "dreams are our imagined possibilities of what might be—they are the key to our identity."

Schlossberg asks: Do women submerge their dreams for their husbands? Does the midlife transition become a crisis if an individual realizes his or her dream has been submerged? The re-evaluation of the dream occurs at marked times, like retirement or death of a loved one. Schlossberg notes that Daniel Levinson's report on his pioneer study of middle-aged men reveals that these men devote a great deal of energy to building a dream. This means that an individual pursues one line of work, one life-style—other options, other women, are ruled out. As time goes on, there is a creeping consciousness, a grieving over lost opportunities, and a process of disillusionment sets in, complete with "what ifs" and "if onlys": "What if I had taken the job in Oshkosh?" "If only I had gone to college." Schlossberg notes that this is a time for questioning, perhaps a time for regrets, and a time for thinking about what might have been.

Chapter 2

Myths and Misconceptions about Physical Change

In the 1960s Joan Baez recorded a Bob Dylan song that described the misfortunes of one hapless fellow who may have been middle aged. The song, "It's All Over Now Baby Blue," mentions events in one person's life that range from the mildly amusing to near catastrophic. As Baez tells the tale:

> Your lover who has just walked out your door,
> Has taken all her blankets from your floor.
> The sky too is falling over you,
> And it's all over now Baby Blue.

Dylan's song is probably an allegory. However, more than one person in my experience has reacted to the onset of middle age as though "it's all over now." Rick is a good example:

On his fortieth birthday his wife gave Rick a surprise party, hoping that his friends would "boost his sagging spirits." They did not. One colleague, a 46 year old, had a few drinks and lamented loudly about "middle-aged miseries" and personal unhappiness. Others made jokes about "middle-aged crazies" and physical breakdowns.

A few days later, Rick, who usually got his exercise watching baseball on TV, bought a new jogging outfit, complete with $60 shoes and a multi-colored sweat band. Within a week he was running three miles a day on concrete sidewalks, coming home exhausted and limping, but proudly describing his accomplishments. His regimen lasted three weeks, until he developed a severe problem with his feet.

Some men panic at 40 and try to regain the physical agility of youth, and in the shortest time possible. Women, too, often become depressed over the physical changes of middle age and seek help in beauty aids, health spas, and cosmetic surgery. These people are reacting to a developmental problem that is real enough, but which is magnified by some of the myths and misconceptions about the physical ravages of middle age.

In fiction and in the mass media, treatment of middle age ranges from the comical to the absurd. The movie "Middle Aged Crazy," is entertaining, but it is also misleading. Television programs dealing with this stage of life often leave the impression that the second half of life is unpleasant and uncertain. Television commercials give us a dismal picture of midlife. Models for tooth paste, designer jeans, and ski apparel are usually young, beautiful, sexy, and unknown. But famous over-50 stars like Lloyd Nolan and Martha Raye sell extra-strength denture powder and mild, twelve-hour laxatives. The message is clear.

Popular and self-help literature on this topic is vast, and some of it supports the notion that midlife is a terrible period; one must endure it, but few enjoy it. For example, one 1973 article on the "male menopause" described midlife in men as a time when hormone levels are dropping, heads are balding, parents are dying, job horizons are narrowing, and friends are having their first heart attacks: "The past floats by in a fog of hopes not realized, opportunities not fulfilled, women not bedded, potentialities not fulfilled, and the future is a confrontation with one's own mortality."

While there is a grain of truth in all this, the exclusive emphasis on decline and breakdown is inaccurate and needlessly depressing. Middle age, like other phases of adult life, is a time of biological change, but these changes are not a prelude to disaster.

Physical Growth and Change

Physical changes in the human body are continuous, beginning at birth and ending at death. One need not be a biologist to note with wonder the changes that take place in children and adolescents. Attaining physical maturity is a momentous event, and in some societies the rite of passage to adulthood is marked by the attainment of adult stature and puberty. A brief overview of growth and development in youth and young adulthood will enhance understanding of the biological changes of middle age.

The major physical changes that bring a person to adult status include skeletal growth, altered body composition, muscular growth, and the development of the circulatory and respiratory systems, which contribute to increased strength and endurance. Changes during puberty are also a factor in attaining adulthood, and these changes have profound psychosocial consequences.

By the early teens most people have attained the physical characteristics of an adult, including the capacity to reproduce. Most of the adult physical sex differences become established during this process. Physical growth continues throughout the teens, with some adolescent "growth spurts" during the early years of this period. By age 15 or 16, however, most young men and women have attained 95 percent of their adult height. Further noticeable growth in stature ceases in women at about 18 and in men at about 20.

Concurrent with physical growth, other changes shape the physique of the adult. Muscular development, including increases in size of the muscles, physical stamina, and endurance, continues into the twenties. Speed and coordination also increase during young adulthood. Some distinct differences in muscular development and in physical strength between men and women become clear in the late teens and early twenties. Generally, men become stronger and develop greater speed and better coordination in body movements than women.

Several other changes, including those involving the face, are more subtle. H. A. Katchadourian writes that the "adult face" emerges during this period. The profile of the adult is straighter, the nose projects further, and the jaw is more prominent. These features are generally more marked in men than in women. A little later the hairline of the man may recede while that of the woman remains the same.

Equally important are the changes that take place internally. The muscles of the heart grow and become stronger, the respiratory and circulatory systems achieve greater capacity, and the number of red blood corpuscles and the blood hemoglobin level increase dramatically. All of this is accomplished before age 30. After 30, physical changes come in a different form than during the earlier years of life.

Biologists and medical researchers make two generalizations about physical changes that begin after 30 and accelerate during middle age. The first is that many, but not all, bodily functions decrease gradually over time. This is not really news to anyone. Most middle-aged persons know that they cannot outrun a 20 year old, and most 40 year olds have little need to demonstrate their physical prowess or athletic ability. There are some exceptions of course. One of the "greatest," Muhammed Ali, was still boxing (but growing weary) at 38, and Fritz Von Berg was playing college football at 50, but not counting on being drafted by either of the pro leagues.

Most of the essential functions of the body decline gradually; about 1 percent of the original capacity is lost per year after age 30. This means that we have the reserve capacity to do most things necessary to daily life until about age 120. Some recent reports suggest that losses of essential functions can be slowed down somewhat by proper health habits, appropriate medical services, and good luck.

The second generalization about physical change is that our chance of dying does not increase in proportion to the amount of function lost. According to B. L. Strehler, this was discovered in 1832 by an English insurance actuary, Benjamin Gompertz. The Gompertz law states that our chance of dying doubles every eight years, regardless of the environment in which we live. This means that the chance of dying is 1,000 times greater for a person of 100 than for a person of 25. Strehler writes that if we did not age—if we could keep the physiology of a 15 year old—the human life span would be in excess of 20,000 years. This would mean that our young friends could describe how the pyramids of Egypt were built and gossip about Anthony and Cleopatra.

We age because the cells in our body that cannot replace

themselves either die or lose part of their function each year. This is true of most of the tissues of the body, although some cells are less affected by the passage of time. The nonaging cells include those in the skin, the lining of the digestive system, and circulating cells in the blood. The skin forms a new layer of cells every four or five days, the lining of our intestines is replaced every day or so, and the red blood cells are replaced regularly every four months.

Other body cells, such as those in the liver, replace themselves more slowly. Vital organs and tissues in which cell replacement is either absent or inadequate are the muscles, the heart, and the brain.

Predicting the effects of biological events that occur with age is hazardous. The rate of change and decline will vary greatly depending upon such factors as general health, occupation, environment, and genetic background. Some research on the functions of vital organs according to age groups provides useful information on losses over time. Strehler reports that the lung function index changes markedly between ages 40 and 60. Generally a 40 year old has about 85 percent of his or her lung function (based on volume of air inhaled and expelled in one minute), but this function decreases to about 50 percent by age 60. Barring severe respiratory diseases or injury, the lung function remains at about 40 percent for most people in their eighties. Strehler estimates that the kidney function index (based on blood flow through the kidneys) is also 85 percent of maximum functioning at age 40, drops to 60 percent at age 60, and gradually levels off in the eighties. The cardiac function index (based on blood pumped by the heart), is generally around 90 percent in healthy 40 year olds, and barring serious illness or disease, declines slowly to 60 or 65 percent until age 75 or 80.

The 40 to 60 decades bring some changes that result in some decline in physical prowess and system functions. But in most people these changes are not so marked that normal activities are seriously restricted or lifestyles changed. In fact, because our habits of living change markedly during this period and since the changes are gradual, most middle-aged people adapt to the changes without difficulty.

Changes in Appearance

Several telltale signs of aging appear in middle age. For most of us a look in the mirror reveals that fat is accumulating around the abdomen and on the hips. Many people gain weight after age 35, and from then until the late fifties most men and women find it necessary to watch their waistline. Weight gain may be even more rapid for middle-aged women, who notice that the extra pounds may be unevenly distributed. Men also begin to get flabby around the middle and slow down because of the excess baggage.

The middle-aged man's hairline begins to recede, hair becomes thinner, and bald spots often appear on top of the head. The beard grows slower, but hair, often as coarse as bristles, appears in the nose and ear. Women's hair may also become thinner and hair may appear on the upper lip and chin. Both men and women tend to have gray hair by age 50 and some by the late thirties.

In their work on the biology of aging, O. J. Selmanowitz and his colleagues write that changes in the bones and in connective tissues contribute further to changes in appearance in middle age. The skin becomes thinner and flatter when it is constantly exposed to the environment. The face, hands, and forearms in particular may change their color as a result of long exposure to sun and wind.

Some striking changes may occur in the shape of the face. The nasal tip gets thicker and the straightness of the nasal profile decreases. The size of the eye opening is diminished and the effect is exaggerated by changes in the nose. The teeth wear down, often become yellowed, and must sometimes be replaced with partial or complete dentures. All of these changes are progressive, of course, and they will be more visible in some people than in others.

It requires little analysis to understand that men and women are concerned about their appearance. The multi-billion-dollar health and beauty industry in this country provides adequate testimony that most people want to look their best. And there are social norms that influence our thinking and behavior on this matter. The extent to which middle-aged people adjust to changes in appearance and other visible signs of aging depends upon social definitions for middle-aged people and their roles, and upon the person's view of herself or himself. Throughout this book I emphasize that the way in which an individual manages to cope effectively with changes and variations in life depends upon how well the person is able to accept his or her own life cycle, and how she or he adapts to external conditions and changes.

Health Changes

Health problems that arise during middle age are quite real and require brief discussion here. Illness can disrupt one's life and cause a reorganization not only in the way one lives but in values and priorities.

Theodore Lidz writes that blood pressure may rise insidiously and that diabetes and heart attacks are much more common in middle age. Heart attacks are a leading cause of death in middle-aged men. Some middle-aged persons begin to notice problems with muscles and joints, and most people begin to tire more easily after age 40.

Some sensory losses become noticeable in middle age. The eyes start to age in infancy but in most people the change is not significant. However, by 50 or 60, a large percentage of the population has corrective glasses. Hearing is at its peak at around age 28 and declines gradually thereafter. Most hearing loss is not noticeable, however, because it involves sounds that are not relevant to behavior.

The extent of these health changes in middle age, and the effect on one's life, depend on heredity, previous health history, work, and lifestyle. Lillian Troll points out that not all changes in health are negative. For example, the frequency of illness goes up with the years, but the frequency of accidents goes down. Adults tend to outgrow some childhood problems and are generally less susceptible to colds and allergies than young people. Middle age does not necessarily bring poor health; the number of disabled people in the 40 to 60 age group is only slightly higher than in young adulthood—about 4.5 percent. Actually, most middle-aged men and women enjoy good health, and many will reach 80 and 90 without being seriously ill or incapacitated.

Sex and Sensuality

In *The Male Mid-Life Crisis,* Nancy Mayer writes that "there comes a time in the life of every American man when his penis is not as playful as it should be." Women, too, are reported to have their problems with sexual activities during middle age. Fiction and popular writing report bleakly on the miseries of menopause and plummeting hormone production during the middle years.

Generalized statements and stereotyped thinking about human sexuality lead to several myths about sexual capacity and sexual activity during middle age. The best evidence does not support the assumption that men lose their virility and women lose their sex appeal during midlife. For most men and women biological changes are not the primary causes of change in sexual interest or ability to perform. Some biological changes occur of course, but sexual behavior in middle age is affected by cultural and psychological factors as well as by biological events. Some discussion of masculine and feminine social roles in contemporary society helps to place this topic in proper perspective.

Men in twentieth-century America are expected to be powerful, healthy, and sexually aggressive. Counselor M. Scher speculates that the man who is not robust, not interested in sports, and not boastful about his sexual exploits may be considered a weakling—not a "real man." Social standards require a man to project himself as tireless, strong, self-assured, successful, and erotic. These demands often cause considerable conflict; nevertheless, men soon get the message that it is desirable to meet these expectations if they are to be viewed as masculine.

Psychologist Harvey Kaye writes that the concept of the powerful male can be attributed to Sigmund Freud, who was certainly a genius, but not infallible. Kaye believes that societal views of the male have developed into a full blown "masculine mystique," which distorts reality and gives rise to several myths about what a healthy man should be. Herb Goldberg, in *The Hazards of Being Male,* describes several "myths about masculinity" that he views as quite harmful to men. He points out that men pay a heavy price for the myth of power and privilege. In fact, millions of men kill themselves trying to live up to society's expectations of a man. Some of these myths relate to a man's sexual needs.

The myth that a man can't get enough sex has been a source of difficulty for many men. According to this myth, men are always ready, "always on the make," and interested mainly "in one thing." We accept the right of a woman to say no, but the man who turns down a beautiful woman may be considered weak, timid, or odd.

A man is not a sex machine; he cannot turn himself on and off any time he has the opportunity for sex. Feelings are important to a man: the person he is with and the circumstances will affect his sexual response.

The joys of sex have been widely heralded and need not be discussed here. But when men take the full responsibility for sex, they risk taking all the joy out of it and turning a pleasant activity into hard work. Some information presented later in this chapter helps to clarify this point.

Myths about the nature of women and the place of women in society are as old as time. In folklore and mythology women were often described as seductive, mysterious, and bewitching; often they were bent upon luring men away from their assigned duties. Woman's sex appeal was so magnetic and her behavior so persistent that men were often powerless to resist. Women's sexual appetites were often so great that men were overpowered; in the presence of a beautiful woman a man might lose his capacity to reason and become her slave.

That image has undergone several modifications over time, of course, but the stereotype of women as sex objects persists in the twentieth century. Cecilia H. Foxley has summarized the work of several researchers regarding sex role stereotypes. She writes in *Nonsexist Counseling* that women are expected to be mainly interested in finding a husband and rearing a family. Women are nurturant, caring, and compassionate. The pre-eminent roles of women are mother, teacher, and nurse. Major features of the female role are beauty, sexual attractiveness, and availability for sex.

These contemporary portrayals of men and women are evidence that society conditions us to fear some normal changes and events in life. The vestiges of that ancient stereotype still tell a woman her most valued qualities are her ability to provide sex, to have children, and to provide attractive companionship—all qualities that are expressed in the context of youth, physical beauty, and fertility. When women age they are viewed as less physically attractive, less fertile, and less sexually desirable. Men also lose some of their youthful vitality, their physical attractiveness, and their "macho" during midlife. Thus, many of the ways that our culture describes successful, attractive, and valuable adults do not hold up with aging. It is no wonder, then, that many people dread middle age.

Sexual Changes in Men

The onset of aging in men is often most personally revealed in the way they change sexually. One 48-year-old male described a change he noticed in himself:

When I was younger, and for the first few years after we were married, I was ready for sex any time, day or night. I could get it up at a minute's notice. We used to make a 400-mile automobile trip every month or so, and I would get horny on the way. More than once I can remember we would stop at a roadside park and make love in the car. Just like when we were teenage kids. Now I don't want it so much. In fact, Lois (wife) sometimes has to take the lead. But I like that. We have sex, oh, two times a week maybe, but I don't get excited as often now.

During midlife several hormonal changes occur in both men and women. This is the menopause in women, and what is sometimes called the climacteric in men.

In men the biological change occurs in the level of production of testosterone, the primary sex hormone, which is responsible for secondary sex characteristics and fertility. J. Wagenvoord and P. Bailey in *Men, A Book for Women,* describe testosterone as a chemical messenger of the body. It is produced in the testes, enters the bloodstream, and travels throughout the body. Testosterone promotes growth and maturation of the male reproductive system and stimulates muscular development. As the level of testosterone increases during adolescence, the penis enlarges, the adolescent growth spurt begins, and secondary sex characteristics, including a beard, emerge. Most sex researchers describe the link between testosterone levels and sexual ability and note that men peak sexually around the late teens and early twenties.

Testosterone production declines slowly after age 20, but most men produce measurable quantities of this hormone throughout their lives. Certainly, testosterone production during the middle years remains at a level sufficient for frequent sex activity and for fertility. Thus, as noted earlier, some of the information on the middle-aged male's sexuality is sketchy and simplistic. For example, research by Masters and Johnson, as well as the earlier work of Kinsey, reveals only a slight decrease in sexual interest over time. Eric Pfeiffer and his colleagues at Duke University found that many men remained sexually active into their seventies and eighties. This does not mean that there is no decline in sexual activity. Most 50-year-old men probably have less sex than men who are 30. By age 50, however, a man surely must know that masculinity is not just in the loins.

Another common myth about male virility is that treatment with extra testosterone will restore waning sexual vigor. In fact, according to James Wagenvoord and Peyton Bailey, except for a temporary benefit, the opposite is true. Extra hormone will diminish, not enhance, sexuality because it has a depressing rather than a stimulating effect on the testes. This is because certain cells in the region of the brain called the hypothalamus record the level of testosterone in the blood. When additional hormone is introduced the testosterone-sensing cells signal the testes to stop production for a while, and it is not until hormone levels even out that the testes resume their work of producing the sex hormones again.

Lidz provides a medical perspective on how hormone production affects male sexuality. Hormonal influences are present not only in the gender orientation of children and in the sex-related behaviors of adolescents, but throughout life. There is some evidence that male hormone production fluctuates in a manner similar to the fluctuation that occurs in women during the monthly cycle.

It should be noted here that while the best scientific evidence on middle-aged sexuality explodes some myths, several questions about sexual capacity and interest remain unanswered and additional research would be desirable. Nevertheless, it is worth repeating that several valid studies reveal that sexual problems in middle-aged men may be more related to psychological factors than to biological events.

Impotence. Impotence has been described as a male plague that becomes critical during midlife. Many men fear it, and most men have experienced it at some point in life. If it happens once or twice it can be embarrassing and frustrating; if it happens often it can be devastating.

Some of the traditional beliefs about impotence were based on myths about masturbation and sexual excesses. In the Victorian era and even into this era, boys and young men were warned that "spilling the fluid" by hand would weaken the system, destroy sexual ability, and interfere with the noble pursuits of manhood. One version of this tale linked insanity to "self abuse." Too much sex was also bad for one's health. Overindulgence would not only weaken the male, but would diminish virility and lead to impotence. This myth may persist. Lillian Rubin, in *Women of a Certain Age*, describes the attitude of one middle-aged woman who has an impotent husband. The woman suspects that he was a sexual athlete as a young man, and now he has burned himself out. She feels cheated and frustrated; just when she feels like a sexual being, he cops out. It is one of "life's rotten tricks."

Technically, there are two kinds of impotence. *Primary* impotence means never being able to get an erection, either by masturbation or in anticipation of intercourse. This condition is quite rare as well as medically complex and will not be discussed here. Most men can and do become erect under proper conditions. In *secondary* impotence the man has "lost his power" or his ability to get an erection on a specific occasion. In the vast majority of cases the problem is psychological.

Much of the literature on the man's inability to achieve or sustain an erection traces the cause to some unconscious fear in the male. Fear of failure, fear of ridicule, fear of getting caught, and anxiety over the size or appearance of the penis have all been cited as factors in impotency. Fear, anxiety, and previous experiences have a basis in reality, but other causes must also be considered. Impotence may in fact reveal a man's feelings about his relationship with the woman he is in bed with. Or, the time may not be right and the man may have other things on his mind. Some men find it difficult to say, "I don't want to make love to you," or "I don't feel like it." Thus, they let the woman believe impotence is the problem.

In a discussion titled "The Wisdom of the Penis," Goldberg points out that men risk sexual suicide when they buy into the notion that they must be able to perform in bed at any time and that impotency is a *man's* problem. The penis may sometimes be wiser than the intellect. The man may have detected rejection, hostility, or anger in his partner, and "making love" becomes difficult or impossible under these circumstances. Sadness, grief, and depression may also cause impotence, and men should not force themselves into sexual acts during such periods.

Many sex therapists agree with Goldberg that the role of the woman is quite important in male sex performance—that men should not feel totally responsible for success or failure in sexual performance. The behavior of the woman, both in and out of bed, can maintain and restore sexual adequacy, or it can destroy a man's sexual capacity and sexual self-image.

Pat is feeling guilty about the increasing incapacity of her 39-year-old husband to perform sexually:

"Our sex life was pretty good, you know, until the last year or so. Then, just when I wanted it more, he seemed to lose interest. I had my tubes tied when I was 36 because we had decided not to have any more children. I thought, wow, this will be great now that we don't have to worry about the side effects of the pill or getting pregnant. But it hasn't worked out that way. He kept taking longer to get excited and sometimes he would only be half hard. Once I told him to hurry up and be a big man and he just shriveled up. At first I kidded him and told him I loved him, no matter what. Then I tried getting him to bed earlier, and I have tried to get him to drink a little before bed, but none of that worked. I don't think I have handled that too well."

In this case the man has been placed on the defensive and made to feel inadequate. He may love his wife, but his sexual desire is stifled because of her attitude toward his performance.

There is yet another issue that bears discussion here. When men accept the myth that they will lose their virility during the middle years, the myth becomes a self-fulfilling prophecy. The male may be unable to get an erection because he has been told that after 50 men do not have strong erotic impulses. A colleague's experience is a case in point:

Alex was a 57-year-old widower with a 24-year-old woman research assistant. They had a good relationship that included an occasional lunch and sometimes a drink after work. As Alex described the progress in the relationship, "the good feeling at work led to dinner, hand-holding, good night kissing, and finally a weekend at the beach. On the way there I had all kinds of fantasies. I was looking forward to a good time; I was sure I would be a terrific lover. I have had a subdued sex life for the last five years. In fact, I have been in bed with a woman only three times since Margaret died. She was an old acquaintance from way back, and about my age I think. So I haven't played around much, and I was looking forward to a weekend in the bed and in the sun. But when we were in the room and I saw her undressed and saw how young she was, I thought: 'What the hell are you doing here old man?' I tell you I got nervous as hell when I thought of my knobby knees and my fat belly; I wondered if I would have a heart attack and be found naked and dead here in a strange town. I tried for an hour but I couldn't get it up. She got dressed and went for a long walk on the beach. I felt like hell, you know, and I realized then I was too old for that kind of playing around so I didn't try again."

Alex may have a good case of performance anxiety, but his remarks about his age are also revealing. A voice in his head is saying that old men with ugly knees and a paunch aren't supposed to be in bed with young women.

Yet male sexual changes in midlife are by no means all negative. Several positive aspects of male midlife change are reflected in the man's sex life. At 45 or 50 erection will take longer to achieve—minutes perhaps, as opposed to seconds in youth. But erection can be maintained for a longer period, and as Masters and Johnson found, premature ejaculation, a common problem in young men, is rare in middle age.

After 40 a man's sexual pleasure changes from a strongly genital to a more diffused experience. Middle-aged people tend to have longer periods of sexual activity than in youth. At midlife, men may not make love as often as younger men, but perhaps they don't need to. By 40 or 50 most men know that sex is only one way to express deep emotions—one of the important things that time alone can teach.

Sexual Changes in Women

Menopause. Biological changes in the reproductive system of women after 40 to 45 are more dramatic than changes in men; and traditionally these changes in women have been viewed as psychologically hazardous. Folklore perpetuated the myth that menopause was a pretty horrible event and that a woman was fortunate if she got through it without becoming terribly depressed or even a little insane. The physical symptoms were amplified to the point that some women expected to be bedridden during the "change of life."

Another common myth among both men and women was that the menopause signaled the end of sexual enjoyment and perhaps even sex activity. These myths have no basis in fact. The reverse may be true, at least for a large percentage of women. In midlife some of the old cultural burdens including guilt, repression, and fear are cast out, and a new and more complete sex and sensuality can be developed.

Cessation of menstruation and loss of the reproductive function is a major landmark in the lives of women, but the biological change is only one of the several changes that occur during this period. Williams points out that the symbolic meaning of menopause invests it with significance that extends far beyond its biological definition. The biological change occurs at a time when women are confronting other changes in life, including changes in appearance, role changes, and changes in lifestyle. Thus, while menopause is a sign of change in the body, climacteric describes a change in life, including perhaps a re-evaluation, and a change in values, goals, and self-perception.

The menopause occurs at an average age of 48, but it may occur in the early or mid forties, and most women begin to prepare psychologically for it after 40. Lidz reports that the menses may taper off over a year or two with a period sometimes missed, or the flow may cease abruptly. The change in hormonal secretions, with the marked decline in estrogen secretion at the start of the menopause, may produce an array of physical discomforts that varies in degree and duration from individual to individual. Lidz explains that while some women report little or no discomfort, many experience "hot flashes," headaches, and dizziness. Most women are simply uncomfortable, but a few may become severely upset. The physical discomforts of menopause can be treated with estrogen replacement therapy. Medical treatment of menopause, however, varies according to the opinions of the physician.

Neugarten and her associates studied 100 women in an effort to discover their reactions to the menopause. They found varied reactions, but concluded that women in their sample tended to minimize the significance of menopause and "to regard it as unlikely to produce much anxiety or stress." Only 4 of the 100 women regarded menopause as a major source of worry, and when asked to identify what they disliked most about middle age, only one woman mentioned the menopause.

Neugarten was interested in how menopause affects sexual activity. She discovered that 65 percent of the women in her study reported no effect on sexual life, and of the 35 percent who reported change, half thought their sexual life had improved and half reported sex as less important. Rubin's study of 160 women between the ages of 35 and 54 reveals findings consistent with Neugarten's report. Rubin states that most women in midlife report that sex has "gotten better and better." Over half of the married women in Rubin's study have sex once or twice a week, and another 20 percent do so three or four times a week. Close to 90 percent achieve orgasm much of the time. Rubin discovered that almost two-thirds of the women in her study engage in oral genital sex, and almost half of them consider it a standard part of their sexual repertoire.

Psychological Reactions to Biological Change

Although many widely held beliefs about physical change in middle age have been shown to be myths, at the same time it must be noted that some biological events of this era will require adjustments in behavior and in lifestyle. Both men and women must deal with changes in appearance in their physical bodies, and they must learn to deal with the reactions of their social group to these changes. Beauty aids and clothing that covers up the signs of aging are now used to great advantage by many people. And so long as society favors youth and rewards people for the way they look, the logical middle-aged person will make a reasonable effort to maintain the most favorable appearance. People who can camouflage some of the signs of middle age probably adjust more rapidly to it.

The exterior changes in the human body are paralleled by changes in internal organs and in the way the organs function. The change in the various organ systems occurs because the process of repair and renewal slows down. Weight gain, bifocals, and sore muscles and joints are all signs of middle age. While most middle-aged people can do most of the things they have always done, they may not be able to do so as rapidly, nor can physical activity be sustained for a long period without fatigue. Longer rest periods may be necessary.

In chapter 1 the concept of developmental tasks in middle age was described. Erikson uses the term "generativity" to describe how middle-aged people begin to concern themselves with teaching the next generation. He maintains that mature men and women need to be needed, and that during middle age their interests and values change and expand to include nurturance and assistance to those who will follow them. Middle-aged adults direct some of their energies in ways that produce some lasting accomplishments or a legacy for the future.

Psychologist Robert Havighurst, too, describes how middle-aged people shift some of their attention toward others and assist youth in becoming responsible adults. Many a middle-aged person becomes a "mentor" or a teacher or a sponsor for a younger person.

One middle age adjustment, according to Robert Peck, is that the person comes to value wisdom over a youthful appearance and physical strength. Peck believes that it is wise to accept the change in physical prowess and learn to use one's wisdom and experience to a greater advantage. He defines wisdom in broad terms as intellectual perception, imagination, and the ability to make good choices. Peck cautions that people who cannot or will not make the transition from physical prowess to wisdom may end up frustrated, bitter and depressed.

One of the critical adjustments that both women and men must make during the second half of life is to changes in sexual functioning. For some men the normal waning of sexual desire may prove frightening. Some men become so concerned about loss of virility that they seek to recapture their powers of youth through liaisons or permanent relationships with younger women. Others understand what is happening, know this is a change and not the end of their sexual life, and adjust to it.

Most women are prepared for the biological changes that accompany menopause, but some are not prepared for the psychological changes that occur at this time. Some women experience depression with the loss of the generative function. This is particularly so for a woman whose sense of womanhood and usefulness is based upon physical attractiveness and her ability to attract members of the opposite sex.

The best evidence on sexual adjustment in middle age is that for a large number of men and women sex is more satisfactory than during earlier periods of life. Sex is often described as more natural and less frenzied, and both men and women report that they have found new ways of satisfying each other. With greater skill and more experience, the sexual act becomes more pleasurable.

One potential problem in sexual adjustment should be noted. Women often report a heightened sexual drive after the menopause. This may be due to a release from the fear of pregnancy and a greater sense of freedom that comes with middle age. Men, who may be experiencing change in their sexual needs, may not always respond adequately to their partner's interest. This may lead to some frustration and cause both men and women to seek new sexual relationships. As noted earlier, their is no reason that most men in their middle years cannot perform sexually under the right conditions. But couples may have to work at understanding each other's total needs, as well as sexual needs, in order to develop harmonious relationships.

The best adjustment to middle age is made by people who openly admit to changes in themselves and who are willing to face the future. Previous experiences and one's view of life in general also affect the way a person adapts to events and transitions during the life span. If we have achieved a sense of identity and a sense of worth by the time we enter middle age, the transition to the second half of life will be smoother and perhaps shorter. A sense of accomplishment in work, in the home, and in the community is also a factor in adjustment to aging. Finally, if a person has the security and the happiness of an intimate relationship, he or she is more likely to make a successful transition to middle age, because that support and understanding can help a person deal with the changes and events that come between 40 and 60.

Chapter 3

The Myth of Intellectual Decline

> I entertained an ex I know
> The moon was high and the lights
>   were low;
> He got dressed up fit to kill
> In the uniform he wore at Bunker Hill.
> He's too old . . . too old, he's too old
>   to cut the mustard any more.

The Bill Carlisle song "Too Old to Cut the Mustard" is a satirical statement on the pitfalls of aging. The Rosemary Clooney and Marlene Dietrich rendition of this 1951 hit reveals some of the nonsensical thinking about intelligence in middle age and later life. The false idea that a person loses mental vitality after 40 is destructive to the individual and leads to stereotyped thinking about people who are middle aged.

A myriad of factors define the individual adult, and one of these factors is called intelligence. Intelligence, however, is an elusive concept. Behavioral scientists offer several and sometimes conflicting definitions for this "something" called intelligence. James Horn, for example, states that almost everyone talks as though he knows what intelligence is: it is something he has in abundance, not something others are lacking. Horn goes on to point out that intelligence has something to do with thinking, problem solving, reacting, communicating, and adapting. Intelligence is not necessarily, as many people think, the critical factor in achievement, earning money, or "doing well." Indeed, several studies reveal that the major differences between people in life achievement, including income, prestige, and education, are due more to factors of circumstance and luck than to intelligence.

The textbooks are not quite sure what intelligence is, but they often lead us to believe that whatever it is declines with age. One grows "too old to cut the mustard" after 40. This means, in folklore, that he or she is probably stranded intellectually—unable to keep the brain working properly and too old to grasp new ideas. Millions of people believe "you can't teach an old dog new tricks" and settle down to conform to the dictates of this myth. But this myth is untrue and should not be an excuse for failure to learn at any period of life.

There are other good reasons why we should dispel the myths about age and intelligence. Many adults, middle aged and older, have felt the weight of discrimination and deprivation because of age. They have been deprived of jobs, denied promotions and salary increases, and dismissed from jobs because someone mistakenly believed they were less productive and less valuable than younger persons. In a period when opportunities for new careers and new lifestyles are greater than ever, some middle-aged people are reluctant to explore new fields or to experience new ways because they have accepted the evaluation of society. After 40, middle-aged people are told, it is time to settle down and accept life as it is. Nothing could be more wrong and more destructive. But it is difficult to chart a new course in the face of this myth. Consider the case of the 42-year-old woman talking with an academic adviser about returning to school.

After twenty years of raising children and keeping house I feel stale and out of touch. But I am restless, and want some intellectual challenge . . . some stimulation. I would like to try college again, but that idea scares me. I know I'm not as smart as I was at 20 and I may have trouble keeping up with young people, but I am willing to work twice as hard. My neighbor tells me I am too old for this, but I want to do something that I like in the years I have left.

To return to college, change a career, or establish new relationships at midlife is difficult enough. One does not need the extra burden of feeling unintelligent. But all too often that is the unpleasant result of a belief in the myth.

Measuring Intelligence

What do we know about changes in the intellect over the life span? How do we measure intelligence? How valid are intelligence tests?

It is questionable whether many of the widely used intelligence tests really measure mental ability. Most probably measure skill at taking tests and the ability to remember what is taught to children and adolescents. That is why many adults do poorly on them. Nevertheless, for years our thinking about mental abilities in adults has been influenced by information gathered by the use of I.Q. (intelligence quotient) tests.

Two approaches have been used to gather information on adult intelligence: one is cross-sectional and the other is longitudinal. The cross-sectional approach studies a random number of people in different groups at successive age levels, while the longitudinal method studies the same people over a period of years. In the 1920s, E. L. Thorndike, an influential American psychologist, used the cross-sectional approach in one of his studies on adult learning. He compared 20 year olds to 40 year olds and so on, and reported a peak in learning capacity at age 22 and a slow but steady decline thereafter. Several years later, D. Weschler, who developed a widely used intelligence test, reported that adults reached their peak performance on intelligence tests in their early twenties and began a gradual decline thereafter.

Cross-sectional research methods such as those used by both Thorndike and Weschler are now suspect, because they do not take into account the fact that the younger generation is better educated and has been out of school for a shorter time than older people. Too, many of the tests are timed and do not reflect changes in visual and motor abilities in people over 30.

Longitudinal studies, several of which have been completed since those cited above, reveal a more positive picture. N. Bayley and M. H. Oden, for example, reported in the *Journal of Gerontology* that under favorable conditions, intelligence may grow until after middle age. According to these researchers, longitudinal studies reveal that in such areas as social intelligence, logical reasoning, interpersonal competence, and technical skill, intellectual growth continues through young adulthood and middle age.

Research on intellectual change over the life span reveals that there are two general categories of intelligence: one increases during the adult years while the other declines. Horn and Cattell used more than thirty mental ability tests to measure the performance of adults over age 50. They discovered one set of abilities that did not decline with time in the 50 to 75 age range, a second set of abilities that did decline with aging, and a third set of abilities that did not fit either category, but depended on such variables as visual and auditory acuity.

The two groups of mental abilities that these researchers categorized as *fluid intelligence* and *crystallized intelligence* are as follows:

Fluid Intelligence	Crystallized Intelligence
Inductive reasoning	Verbal comprehension
Figure matching	Mechanical knowledge
Memory span for numbers or	Arithmetic ability
nonsense syllables	Fluency of ideas
Perceptual speed	Experimental evaluation
	General information

Crystallized intelligence is the collective ability of a society, passed on from one generation to the other by parents and teachers, through written information, and by learning from experience. This ability grows rapidly during childhood and adolescence, and then more slowly during the adult years. Individual variations in adulthood are great. Havighurst believes that after age 60 crystallized intelligence only increases in people who are intellectually active.

Fluid intelligence consists of those abilities that depend most directly on the physiological structure of the organism and especially the central nervous system. Fluid intelligence declines over time, beginning at around age 30. Havighurst states that the neural structures of the central nervous system grow during infancy and childhood, and may decline thereafter. For example, the speed of reaction to a touch on the back or to a light signal decreases. The decline becomes marked after age 50 to 55.

While reaction time, computational speed, and short-term memory may show some decline with age, there is a trade-off. At age 45, for example, the average person's vocabulary is three times as great as at age 20. The brain of a 60 year old possesses almost four times as much information as it did at age 21. Thus, wisdom and maturity may compensate for speed and sharpness.

K. Warner Schaie, a psychologist who has spent more than twenty years studying adult intelligence, summarized his findings in a 1979 report. He states that decrements in intelligence may not show up until old age (the late eighties). He maintains that in most healthy people change in intellectual ability in middle adulthood and later life is relatively small and probably does not affect their lives. (Decreases are likely to be found in people with severe cardiovascular disease beginning in the late fifties and early sixties.) What does decline is speed. With age people tend to take more time on test items, and they do not react positively when they are urged to hurry.

Researchers have been misled as a result of their failure to look closely at adult mental abilities. The notion that at 60 or any other age, adults become incompetent or senile is ludicrous. Our obsession with youth has led us to believe that after middle age one is "out of it." This bit of nonsense has caused society to lose some of its best brain power. Middle age does not mean that one has reached a dead end or a plateau. It is a time when experienced, mature people can use all their capacity for continued growth. It is also a time when accumulated skills and experiences can be used for the betterment of society.

Learning

> Ah, nothing is too late
> 'Til the tired heart shall cease to palpitate.
> Cato learned Greek at eighty;
> Sophocles wrote his grand Oedipus and Simonides

Bore off the prize of verse from his compeers
When each had numbered more than fourscore years.
Henry W. Longfellow

As a person ages, he or she has not only the ability to learn, but more training in the skills of learning. Fifty year olds can learn the same things as 15 year olds. The belief that at 50 or 60 one is an inept old fogy is a myth. The passage of time has little effect on the ability to perform the tasks of middle age. In fact, by this time in life, our experiences and good sense begin to really count. Henry Thoreau wrote: "The youth gets together materials for a bridge to the moon, and at length the middle-aged man decides to make a woodshed with them."

Living in modern society requires that a person learn a series of complex tasks, and keep on learning throughout life. According to Havighurst, in simple unchanging societies people may have mastered most necessary learning tasks by early adulthood. For those individuals most learning is over because there is little else one needs to know, and because society changes so slowly. Not so in a society where social life changes so rapidly that the individual must learn new things continually in order to keep up with the times. This has probably been so for the past 100 years at least. How, then, does one explain the absurd notion that one stagnates after 40 or 50? The answer to this question is not totally clear, because we still do not know enough about the effects of aging. But we do know that people change physically. It has thus been easy to generalize about mental change and age.

Our society has also treated people as objects, and when people aged they were often viewed as ineffective; in the workplace they were fired to make way for younger, more productive people. While this condition has changed somewhat in recent years, our youth-conscious society continues to display some hostility and considerable ignorance about people over 50.

Furthermore, some earlier conclusions on adult learning were based on studies that were poorly conceived and inaccurately interpreted. Publication of the results of these studies has had some negative effects upon middle-aged and elderly people.

In a preceding paragraph I cited the Thorndike study of adult learning in which he concluded that learning capacity reached a peak at age 22 and began a steady decline thereafter. His approach was cross-sectional, comparing young people with old people over the same period of time. Thorndike focused attention upon how fast adults learn rather than upon how accurately and how much they learn. Some of his measures of learning were questionable. For example, one measure was how fast right-handed people could write with the left hand, how fast a person could decipher a code, and how fast one could learn to use an artificial language.

Thorndike wrote voluminously on age and learning. Unfortunately many psychologists and educators accepted his findings and helped perpetuate the myth that after young adulthood we fall off the edge intellectually. Some adults, believing that they are supposed to grow stupid after 40, give up and resist trying anything new. Others, realizing the prejudice and shallowness in this kind of thinking, go out and prove the "experts" wrong. A 1981 news story illustrates this point.

KALAMAZOO, Mich. (UPI)—Lina Marshall, 85, Saturday received a Bachelor of Arts degree in Religion at Western Michigan University.

Mrs. Marshall, who pledged the Phi Mu sorority last year—making her the oldest sorority member in Western's history—was born in 1895, seven years before the university was founded.

In brief remarks to her 1,175 classmates, she said, "Dare to be different."

"Don't be limited by society and its stereotyping and false notions about aging," she said. "I suggest that you can make your later years as rewarding and fulfilling as your earlier years."

"But you must have a plan for the goals and a desire to achieve something," she said, adding, "I had a plan."

Mrs. Marshall is from Benton Harbor, Mich. (*Daily Progress*, Charlottesville, VA., April 26, 1981)

During the past two decades, several researchers have pointed out the fallacy in some traditional thinking about aging and learning. J. C. Zahn, for example, states in *Adult Education* that the basic ability to learn changes little with age and that such changes as do occur are not changes in ability, but changes in physical state including disease, and changes in interests, motivation, and in ways of viewing experience. This view is consistent with research findings of M. W. Lawrence, who reports that older adults see little point in learning something that is useless or meaningless. Thus, interest and motivation are important factors in adult learning.

In a period of rapid social and technological change it is imperative that learning continue throughout life. In childhood, one learned to read and to participate in social activities because of cultural pressure. In adult life the person learns complex work skills and masters the tasks of daily living. In this century adults have learned to live in a world of advanced technology and rapid change. Changes in one's life over the years are additional sources of learning.

C. B. Aslanin and H. M. Brickell conducted a nationwide survey on life change and learning. They identified several transitions in adult life that stimulate or require people to continue learning. Life transitions such as changing jobs, advancing in a career, getting married, getting divorced, retirement, and death of a family member are all triggers to adult learning. Aslanin and Brickell maintain that learning is a "reorienting experience," which can provide new opportunities and new directions at any age.

What can we now conclude about middle age and learning? We can discard the myth about teaching an old dog new tricks, because it is never too late to learn. It is clear that when learning is measured without strict time limits, learning ability does not decline between the ages 20 and 60. As Zahn writes, persons who are bright at 20 do not become dull at 60. At 60 a person can learn the same kinds of knowledge and skills he could at 20.

Malcolm Knowles, an authority on adult learning, tells us that from adulthood to middle age ability to learn does not decline. Performance on some tests may show a decline because of lower motivation, speed, or a loss of vision or hearing. Growing older does not change the ability to learn or to think. Growing older does change one's interests, values, goals, and motivation. These changes may affect how one learns and what one learns, but not the ability to learn.

Creativity and Productivity

Youth is a time of getting and middle age a time of improving, writer Anne Bradstreet has said. If you stay active you will also stay smart, and at 60 you can demonstrate that you have not grown older, but better.

George Bernard Shaw, a noted British dramatist, wrote his first play when he was 36 years old and continued his work as a writer and critic until his death at 94. Josephine Baker, the singer from St. Louis, was an active performer for more than fifty years. She gave four concerts in Carnegie Hall when she was 66. Ronald Reagan entered politics in his late fifties and ran for a second term for president of the United States at 73.

While it is true that creative activities in many people tend to peak in the late thirties or early forties, the peak varies with different professions. H. C. Lehman studied aging and achievement and reported the ages for maximum creativity in several professions. Grand opera, 35 to 39; musical comedy, 40 to 44; chemistry, 26 to 30; mathematics and physics, 30 to 34; astronomy, 40 to 44; writing novels, 40 to 44; writing short stories, 30 to 34; writing poetry, 24 to 39; painting and sculpture, 32 to 39; architecture, 40 to 44; inventions, 39 to 40; and economics, 35 to 39.

Though some people may peak early, creative people tend to remain creative throughout life. John McLeish, in his book *The Ulyssean Adult*, states that for the well-conditioned mind there is no upper limit. He provides numerous examples of well-known works completed by people in their fifth, sixth, seventh, and eighth decades of life. McLeish also maintains that the retirement years can be a most productive period, when creative drives that have been stifled for years can be unleashed.

Brilliant ideas and the capacity to create do not desert the brain or body after middle age. Thus, the notion of non-creativity and low productivity in older people is largely a myth. For some there is probably a middle age slowing down, just as there is some decline in physical stamina and endurance, but there are numerous examples of the flowering of creative talents after midlife. And this is a most logical period for the development of creative talents.

Young adults are usually heavily involved in such developmental tasks as selecting a career, marrying, and raising children. These are all time consuming and socially required activities. People are expected to "make it" or "get ahead" by middle age, and they may have little time to pursue personal interests. But by age 40, as we have seen, many people begin to re-examine their lives and change directions. They may discover that success and satisfaction do not necessarily come with financial security and social status. They seek other means of self-realization. Count Leo Tolstoi, Russian novelist and philosopher, became disillusioned with commercialism and materialism in his middle years and changed his views about his country, society, and his own lifestyle. Some of his most important works appeared after his fiftieth birthday.

When he was almost 50 years old, historian Dumas Malone decided that he should write "a big book about Thomas Jefferson." He finished his book three years later and continued writing about the third president of the United States. In 1974 when Mr. Malone was past 80, his fifth volume on the sage of Monticello appeared, and the series won the Pulitzer Prize in History. Mr. Malone completed his final volume on Jefferson at age 89 and thinks now that he may "write up" the story of his travels with Mr. Jefferson. Mr. Malone noted that the idea for the work on Jefferson was conceived early, but that it was not until after age 50 that he was able to devote a major portion of his time to it.

Creativity and productivity throughout life are not limited to writers, artists, or college-educated professionals. Millions of people who work in factories, on farms, and in offices continue employment and creative output until 80 or 90. They continue to learn new skills, to improve their techniques, and to participate actively in community, religious, and professional affairs.

Myths about intellectual decline, learning stagnation, and shrinking productivity during middle age are interlocking stereotypes that defy reality. Middle age can be a time of renewed vigor, heightened productivity, and personal creativity. It is a time when people can begin to do what they want to do with their lives. The brain does not shrink at 40. Such notions are harmful, because they lead to a waste of talent and experience.

MIDDLE-AGE COLLEGIANS

Fifty year olds no longer stand out in a college classroom. In community colleges, four-year colleges, and universities throughout the country men and women in their fifties, sixties, and seventies are pursuing college degrees and special interest programs in record numbers. One Midwestern college admissions director stated: "We have many students over 40, and people in their sixties are a common sight in some of our classes. Computer technology has been responsible for some of that trend, but I think older people have varied interests and they are ready for another classroom experience in later life."

Figures from the National Center for Education Statistics reveal that 22 percent of the current college population is over 30, and 12.8 percent is over 35. The increase in the over-30 college population since 1972 is almost 7 percent.

Chapter 4

Love, Work, and Middle Age

Love makes the world go 'round.

Every man's work shall be made manifest: for the day shall declare it, because it shall be revealed by fire; and the fire shall try every man's work of what sort it is.

I Corinthians 3:13

In his discussion of the Eight Stages of Man, Erikson describes Freud's views on what a normal adult should be able to do well. In his mature years Freud is reported to have stated that the well-adjusted person should be able to "lieben and arbieten" (love and work). Freud probably used "love" to mean genital love and "work" to describe a general work productiveness. But as Erikson notes, he did not mean that work would so preoccupy the person that he or she could not be a loving human being. This chapter deals with the unique meaning of love and work during the midlife period.

Most people find maximum satisfaction and meaning in life only when they are in a caring reciprocal relationship with another person or persons. Love is a critical factor in psychological adjustment, and numerous therapists report that a characteristic of psychologically healthy adults is that they are able to form intimate, loving relationships. In his report on how a group of college-educated men adapted to life over time, Vaillant wrote that "one can live magnificently in this world if one knows how to work and how to love." George and Nena O'Neill, authors of *Shifting Gears,* believe that love relationships are essential to personal growth and achievement. Two people working together can accomplish more in life than either can individually.

It is difficult to give a precise definition of either love or work, but each has some elements that can be identified. M. N. Reedy, J. E. Birren, and K. W. Schaie describe several components of love, including caring, affection, tolerance, respect, common interests, self-disclosure, support, trust, physical and sexual intimacy, and commitment to the future of the relationship. Marjorie Lowenthal and her associates state that the major components of interpersonal intimacy are similarity, reciprocity, and compatibility. Love and intimacy are terms that overlap, almost to the point of fusion; however, some distinctions should be made between love and sexual intimacy. Our culture tends to confuse love and sex and appears at times to equate love and sexual contact. Sex is one of the ways we express our feelings and one of the components of intimacy, but having sex does not mean that we are in love, nor that we are intimate in a real sense. This view is in contrast to Desmond Morris's equation of intimacy with physical contact. Morris describes twelve stages that he claims men and women pass through in order to establish the "bond" of attachment. His final stage is sexual intimacy. Morris points out that physical contact, bonding, and sexual intimacy, while necessary to the survival of the species, are not acts engaged in for that purpose alone. Physical contact and sexual intimacy are natural activities that provide pleasure to both men and women.

Common Elements in Love and Work

Love and work have several common elements: both require commitment and both contribute to personal identity. Nathan Hale suggests that love and work are the two phenomena that make civilized living possible. Young people are expected to establish themselves in a job or career, fall in love, marry, and become parents. Modern society expects people to demonstrate a capacity for love and for work productivity before it grants a person adult status.

Work, perhaps more than any other activity, gives meaning and purpose to life, Studs Terkel tells us in *Working*. Even though

Americans tend to have a love-hate relationship with work, he says, a person deprived of work may lose personal identity and self-respect.

For many people, work involves devotion to an idea, a cause, or an activity. Many people spend most of their time and energy on a vocation or an interest, devoting themselves totally to that activity. One person may spend his or her life in the ministry; another may devote all of his or her life to law and justice, and another to woodcarving or farming. Many of these people love their work, and for them the love-hate dichotomy does not exist.

Recent research on adult living reveals that difficulties in either love or work may result in a decline in mental health. Increased drug use, alcoholism, and negative social attitudes are frequently evident in people who experience failure in these major aspects of life. Some individuals adapt to problems in one of these realms by devoting more time to some other activity. This may be a partial solution or a temporary means for dealing with an unsatisfactory condition or a loss, but it is no real solution for the basic problem. Because love and work are so central in our lives they affect all our behaviors—our sociopolitical attitudes, our feelings about ourselves, our mental health, even the length of life itself.

Developing a Sense of Love and Work

Love

Love and work are realms of life that are influenced significantly by our interactions with our culture. We learn about love and about the behavior of love relationships through contacts with people. Our understanding of work is acquired in a similar way. As we experience love and work we develop individual ways of dealing with these phenomena, and we attach our own personal meanings to each experience. Love and work experiences are developmental processes, beginning in infancy and terminating with death. Raymond Gale, in his book *Who Are You?*, has identified several stages of love that are relevant to this discussion:

Self-love. This stage of love involves having one's own needs met with little regard for others. This self-centered, demanding stage of love is most characteristic of small children; however, some adults display attitudes and behaviors that can be described as self-love.

Love for Parents. Children soon learn that their needs are met by their parents and that they are dependent on parents for food and comfort. They learn to associate feelings of pleasure and security with parents, and as children mature, feelings of love grow beyond themselves to include a mother and father as well.

Love for Other Relatives. After children learn how to love their parents, they develop broader affectional relationships. Developing attachments for siblings, grandparents, and other relatives is an important step in love development. From these experiences, the person learns about trust and reciprocity, which are critical in future relationships.

Love Relationships Outside the Family. When young people begin to explore the world outside the home, they discover new affectional relations among persons their own age. Sometimes these first loves outside the family are the same sex, sometimes the opposite sex. Close relationships with age-mates are an important step in that it means the person forms close ties outside the family. These relationships also give a person confidence and experience in how to develop caring relationships with others.

Love of Opposite Sex, Same Age. Love of the opposite sex usually begins with a generalized feeling, both romantic and erotic, for members of the opposite sex. During adolescence and young adulthood most people have several experiences and infatuations with members of the opposite sex in their age group. Later there is a tendency to focus on one person, followed by "going steady." Some tentative commitments are made at this time, and the commitments may become real if the couple becomes engaged. Developmentally, this process occurs over a period of years, and many people have more than one adult love relationship before marriage.

The research on this topic reveals identifiable patterns in love relationships over time. The intense romantic relationships among newlyweds usually gives way to a more even, and perhaps more realistic, and mutually caring relationship brought on by the necessities of parenting and earning a living. As lovers grow older together relationships have their ups and downs, and some fall apart. But there is evidence also that middle-age relationships develop into deeper levels of commitment and attachment. This topic is discussed in more detail in a succeeding section.

Love for Mankind. Marriage and child rearing provide the most prolonged and most intense love relationships for the majority of adults. Feelings of love for children during this period may at times overshadow affectional relationships with the spouse, and this condition can be a factor in marital unhappiness among the mid-thirties age group. But, as noted earlier, when children are grown, husbands and wives tend to re-negotiate their relationship, and middle-aged people often report new interest in each other and increased happiness in the relationship.

During middle age people who are successful in the sequential pattern of love experiences often develop not only a mature love for family members and close friends, but they are also able to experience deeper feelings and concerns for people in general. By this stage most people have acquired the self-confidence and maturity that make caring for others possible. The person now becomes interested in responsibilities to mankind and in promoting human welfare.

Erikson uses the term *generativity* to describe the mature adult's efforts to assist or guide the next generation. In Erikson's view, mature adults are not only able to apply the generativity drive to their own children, but they are also ready to encourage and assist other young people.

Of course not all people develop the capacity to care for mankind, nor does every adult achieve a sense of responsibility for future generations. The reasons may be found in excessive self-love, a lack of faith in one's power to help others, or in an inability to deal effectively with demands in one's own life.

In this discussion of the last two stages of love, a traditional context of dating, marriage, and child rearing is assumed. This is the usual pattern in adult life. But it is recognized that contemporary society provides alternative styles of living, and some people establish long-term love relationships outside of marriage. In these relationships, the sequential pattern for the development of a sense of love is quite similar to the pattern described above.

Love and Sexuality

The physiological aspects of sexual behavior in the middle years were discussed in chapter 2. While there is little decline in a person's ability to function sexually, as one matures needs and interests change. During the middle years sexuality may have new and different meanings. For example, sex is a means of communicating love and intimacy, but for mature people sex does not necessarily mean intercourse; touching, kissing, and caressing are all sexual expressions.

Some marriage therapists believe that one of the problems of middle-aged people is how to keep sex in the relationship. They report that for some people over 50, sex too often becomes routine, boring, scheduled, and ritualized. Many experts recommend that married couples try to become more imaginative more often, and Alan Tavis and Philip Sadd report that most middle-aged men are pleased to see their wives in lacy lingerie and wearing new perfume. Men are often advised to be more "romantic" and more sensitive to the needs of their partner.

Sexual mores in western society have undergone dramatic change in the past four decades. Movies and television soap operas depict sexual relations as open and casual, and to a degree that view is accurate. The frequency of extramarital sex rises during midlife, and according to some people, solves a need for variety and excitement. Some recent studies dealing with this topic found that up to 75 percent of all married men and 55 percent of all married women over 35 had been involved in at least one extramarital sex relationship. Hunt described adultery as the hidden reality of American life. "The most common attitude toward the extramarital affair is somewhat like the American attitude toward the payment of income tax," Hunt said. "Many people cheat; some a little and some a lot; most who don't would like

SEXUAL LOVE

Several years ago the eminent psychotherapist Rollo May described the values of sexual love. According to May the first is the overall value of enrichment and fulfillment of personality. This comes from the expansion of one's awareness of one's self, one's feelings, and the experience of giving pleasure to another person. This feeling carries us beyond where we are at any given moment: we become, in a literal sense, more than we were.

Tenderness is the second value, a tenderness that is more than "togetherness." It is a tenderness that comes from the fact that two separate people have overcome their separateness and formed a union. In this kind of sexual love the lover does not know whether a particular sensation of delight is felt by himself or herself or by the loved one—and it doesn't make any difference anyway.

There is a third value that occurs ideally at the moment of climax in sexual intercourse. This is the point when the lovers are carried not only beyond their personal isolation, but when a shift in consciousness seems to occur that seems to unite them with nature.

The fourth value in sexual love, according to May, is the affirmation of self. Sexual love is a meaningful way to achieve a sense of personal identity. We emerge from lovemaking with a renewed vitality, a vitality that comes not from triumph or proof of one's strength, but from renewed awareness.

A final value in love making is the ability to give to the other person. This is essential to one's own full pleasure in the act. Just as giving is essential to one's own full pleasure, the ability to receive is necessary in the love relationship, also. If you cannot receive, your giving will be a domination of your partner. Conversely, if you cannot give, your receiving will leave you empty.

to but are afraid; but most people don't admit the truth except to a close confidant." Yet our culture in general does not endorse extramarital affairs. Roper found that both men and women felt that marital fidelity was important, but many admitted they could not live up to their own standards.

Several explanations have been offered for the increase in extramarital involvement in midlife. One perspective holds that fears over declining physical attractiveness and vitality push both men and women to prove that they are still attractive to the opposite sex. Other reasons include boredom, unhappiness, and loss of interest on the part of one's partner. More probably, several factors are necessary to explain extramarital affairs. Throughout this book the self-assessment phenomenon common in midlife has been noted. Thus, when sexual needs and sexual satisfaction are carefully examined, some people may logically conclude that some new approaches to satisfying their needs are appropriate.

Most people who have extramarital sex attempt to conceal the fact from their spouse. Others admit it and try to work through the problems that result. Still other couples overtly agree to have other sexual partners. They do not conform to traditional rules and mores of society. Those people who are comfortable in a sexually open marriage maintain they enter such a relationship because of their great respect for individual rights of expression and primacy. Research data on the success of open marriages is sparse; however, at least one book on this topic maintains that a few couples have found this arrangement quite satisfactory.

During middle age sexual activity tends to become integrated with intimacy—sexuality may take on new meaning, and the sexual aspects of the relationship may be redefined. Sex becomes not just a biological function, but an expression of closeness, caring, and continued commitment.

Work

Several social scientists have identified specific stages in the development of a sense of work and in the way people experience work over the life span. Donald Super, for example, describes five stages of career development extending from childhood to old age. The focus here is on work and midlife; however, for explanatory purposes, all of Super's stages are briefly defined.

Growth Stage. The person's first experience with work occurs during childhood. The home and the school provide several opportunities to learn that people perform a variety of jobs and hear adults discuss their interests and their work. Children learn about the jobs men and women do, and young people have an opportunity to think about some of the things they would like to do when they grow up.

The Exploratory Stage. During the teenage years the school and the community provide opportunities for people to explore a work future as well as interests, values, and beliefs. In fact, secondary schools may be properly viewed as exploratory in both purpose and content. The curriculum, special programs, and part-time jobs are all important in helping young people make decisions about their future life and their work.

The Establishment Stage. Our society expects people to settle down, find a job, marry, and establish a home in their twenties or early thirties. Exploration in jobs is usually over by age 30 or earlier, and the person now attempts to find a satisfying job and settle into it.

Super writes that the young person seeking a place in the world of work is in fact looking for more than a job; the person is attempting to implement a self-concept. Work is more than earning a living; it is verification of the self. Having tried out a variety of jobs, the young adult now has some insight about work and about personal interests and needs. At this point many men and women make the first major commitment to an occupational goal and to their own future.

Maintenance and Middle Age. By the age of 45 or 50, most people in the professions and the skilled occupations are established in a career. Semi-skilled workers, too, have generally established a place in the work world; however, they may hold a series of jobs over time and experience periods of unemployment as the economy shifts up and down.

Typically, the middle-aged worker does not try to open up new lines of work but concentrates on acquiring greater proficiency and status in his or her chosen field. Middle-aged persons who have been successful may want to hold on to their gains rather than risk them in striving for more success. The person who has not been successful may wonder whether he will ever find a place for himself. Obviously some people change careers during mid-life, and these changes generally grow out of the re-evaluation of all aspects of living. This psychological phenomenon is discussed in detail in the succeeding sections. At this point, Levinson's observations on work and midlife are relevant. He writes that few people achieve all their hopes through work. From the point of view of adjustment or happiness, work at midlife can bring a sense of fruition or frustration. The fruits of long years of work can be accepted and enjoyed, or a sense of failure and despair may emerge.

Decline. The fifth developmental stage of work is described as decline and begins at about age 60. This is the "slowing down" period just before retirement and the period of retirement itself. Adjustment in this stage is related to the previous stages and to adjustment in other realms of living.

Midlife Adjustments to Work and Love

In all societies work is a major aspect of adult life and of the social structure. Every person is expected to be productive and to make a contribution to the social group. For men, work is a primary factor in determining social status, income, and personal identity. By middle age men are expected to be stable, contributing members of society, and society's criteria for judging stability and status are linked to occupations.

For centuries Western society's requirements for women differed significantly from those for men. Until the women's rights movement a large percentage of women spent most of their time in unpaid work and were not required to deal with the work force and its problems. Now that 50 percent of the women in some countries work for wages outside the home, society will need to re-define its expectations and its views on women and work. Even now, work during midlife is a major issue for an increasing number of women.

Traditionally, in our culture love was the ideal as well as an experience. To experience love, to enter a permanent relationship through love and marriage, was a mark of achievement and adult status. The love commitment was one way to verify the person, or in Eriksonian concepts, it helped to fulfill the quest for identity. This love ethic emphasizes obligation, attachment, and "settling down": child rearing, work, and participation in community affairs are important tasks in this adult role. This ethic provides some order and stability for society, but at the same time it has always contained conflicts for some people. An essential element of individual identity is freedom, including the choice of changing directions, changing jobs, or changing marriage partners. Thus, commitments made in love and work may mean loss of freedom and failure in the quest for identity. As Ann Swider states, people may feel trapped or stifled in a marriage: work for some is a loss of freedom, a shameful "settling down."

Men

By midlife most people have assumed a large number of roles and responsibilities. Considerable time and energy is being devoted to a career and the family. Middle-aged men often devote their primary attention to their jobs in order to make new gains and to establish security for their old age. Career achievement and job satisfaction during this period vary with the work and the worker. If the individual is successfully established in an occupation in terms of security, the respect of others, and personal feelings of accomplishment, he may be satisfied and fulfilled in his career. Work satisfaction is often paralleled in the home and in personal relationships. Sharing one's achievements with a spouse and enjoying some of the freedom that comes with middle age is often cited as one of the satisfactions of men over 40.

The picture is quite different for the person who is not established and successful in a career. For the man who does not have stability in work and who finds little satisfaction in a job, midlife is likely to be a period of unhappiness and frustration. Job insecurity, insufficient rewards, and poor relationships with colleagues leads to a sense of discouragement and failure.

As noted earlier, adjustment in one aspect of life affects adjustment in another. Thus, failure at work often strains love relationships. It is difficult to be attentive and responsive when one is preoccupied with work-related problems. In her research with middle-class Americans, Lowenthal discovered that many middle-aged men experience problems in personal relationships, because they are making last ditch efforts to achieve success in work before they retire. She writes that many middle-aged men are so preoccupied with that final promotion or salary increase that they have little energy for anything else.

The man who loses a job at midlife may be in serious trouble. It is often difficult for people over 40 to find jobs, and in a period of economic uncertainty the problem is magnified. The psychological effects of prolonged unemployment are often devastating for men. The unemployed male feels inadequate, frustrated, and angry; he may not be able to support his family and views himself as a failure. He loses status in the eyes of his wife and children, who may turn away from him as his anger and resentment increase. Alcoholism, mental health problems, marital strife, and divorce can result from long-term unemployment.

Women

Women who work outside the home often become as deeply involved with their careers as men. Women, too, make long-term commitments to work and strive for success in their careers. However, many career women will experience the powerful pull to have children several times during their life. Gould believes that this desire for children becomes particularly strong in the thirties when women realize that the childbearing years are coming to an end. Gould states that successful career women may find this a particularly difficult time, because they understand the problem of combining child rearing with a time-consuming career. For women, commitment to a career means a compromise of some other things that society has defined as important. Too, as Rubin has noted, the ability to make a commitment to work outside the home may be contingent on the approval of the husband, especially when there is no pressing financial need for a woman to work. Some women are afraid their marriage will suffer if they work outside the home.

Middle age is a time when a woman who gave up an outside job to marry and raise a family may return to the labor force. It is also a time when some women make their first venture into the world of work. Some women work for economic reasons: to assist children with college expenses, to supplement the family income, and to save for retirement. Many women are the sole support of a family. They have few options and could not stop working if they wanted to.

The women's movement has resulted in many women realizing their goals through work. Changing social attitudes and increased employment opportunities enable more women to combine a career and marriage. Rubin has noted, however, that despite more than a decade of feminist change, middle-aged women still have many doubts and some guilt about making major commitments to work. They are not sure about the independence that comes with a full-time job, and most of all they are concerned about the reactions of their husbands and family. Rubin cites examples of husbands who will not tolerate a working wife, as well as family members who think it's great for mother to work until her schedule begins to interfere with their needs.

Midlife Review of Love and Work

In the middle of their lives people are forced to review their current status and grapple with the question: "How do I wish to live the rest of my life?" In the two most significant areas of living—love and work—they become aware that several transitions are taking place, and that these call for new strategies for living.

I have already noted that in that middle period of life men and women often pause to examine reality. Traditionally, most people accepted the one-spouse-one-career imperative, but that view has changed drastically in this century. Adults now recognize that they are no longer stuck with decisions made early in life, and that opportunities for change still exist at middle age. It is no longer realistic to expect everyone to choose a job or a spouse at age 20 and remain in that line of work or in that relationship for a lifetime. Deviations from this pattern are now common.

Men

In the re-evaluation at midlife, men will attempt to determine whether they have succeeded or failed, moved forward or stagnated, and found happiness or despair in both love and work. Judith Bardwick writes that some men will not like what they have become and will make major changes in their life. In the midst of what some people describe as "male midlife crisis," some men will say, "I have been good, but now I will find pleasure and behave as I please; I have been a work horse, now I will be a stud; I wore tweeds and pin stripes, now I will wear neck chains and body shirts." Nancy Mayer states that some middle-aged men make several dramatic changes that others may consider crazy. But most men will find no lasting solutions in these kinds of changes. A play solution to issues of work is at best superficial, and leaving a wife that one has spent a quarter of a century with may not solve issues of love and intimacy. Thus, a fruitful re-evaluation focuses not only on work and intimate relationships, but involves a complex appraisal of values, psychosocial needs, and goals for the next stage of life.

Many middle-aged men are seeking more freedom and recognition in work and more personal meaning in life. Work is a dominant force and for many a source of identity and satisfaction, but boring, exhausting work produces feelings of anger, frustration, and bitterness. These men direct some of the anger at themselves, because they now recognize that they could have changed their circumstances years before. They still seek opportunity for creativity and self-expression in work, and many of these men are willing to give their best effort to a job that has some personal meaning and adequate financial rewards. Some conclude that they will no longer remain in a job that cheapens their worth and offers few personal satisfactions.

Increasing numbers of men are changing careers after 35. Many more would probably like to, but see no way to implement a change in their present situation.

Steve Harper was a successful businessman at age 44. He was close to the top in a highly competitive field and made enough money to live quite well. But he began to lose interest in the rat race, and the continuous pressure made him anxious and irritable. He described his feelings as "fed up with the organization, and bored with the same old routine." The job held little satisfaction, and he felt trapped in a role. Steve responded to the internal feelings by quitting the job. He moved his family to a rural community and started his own small business.

Lee Isaacson wrote that not all midlife career change comes from self-examination or a chance to realize long held dreams. For many people, career change arises from the nightmare of losing a job. Here the worker doesn't have the option of staying in an old job or trying a new one: instead he is confronted with the necessity of making a change that is unplanned, and frequently disadvantageous. Often the worker finds that other employers in his geographic area have no need for a person with his skills.

Some middle-aged men are forced out of a position—often resigning just before they are fired—because of changes in policies, decisions to relocate, or plans for re-organization. They often leave with feelings of bitterness and with no future career plans.

Isaacson has pointed out that technology has produced many unexpected career changes at all ages. Technical obsolescence may lead to plant closing or automation, and mechanization may reduce the need for workers.

Voluntary career change, particularly when it is carefully planned and implemented, can be a good decision. But involuntary career change is another matter. Most of what we know about work and adult living suggests that a career loss can be a traumatic and devastating experience. The need to identify and enter a new career at the very time when other needs are emerging can create turmoil for the individual. Loss of a career is often accentuated by anger and grief reactions, not easily understood by the individual involved nor by a spouse and children.

Women

Midlife may be the first time that many women have the freedom to attend to their own interests. This is the point in the family life cycle when the children are grown—or nearly so—and when women can begin to think about their own needs and goals. The consciousness-raising efforts of the women's movement have produced large-scale social change, including more independent actions on the part of women.

Research on change in sex roles over the life span reveals that a tendency to more autonomous behavior in middle-aged women may be a result of internal as well as social change. For example, by age 40, many women appear to become more assertive, more managerial, and more dominant in their relationships with men. While their orientation to nurturance and caring for a family remains strong, there is nevertheless a tendency to assume more authority and to make more decisions than during young adulthood.

During the re-evaluation of middle age, women who have lived traditional roles may say, "I have been deprived of roles that I now want. It is now time for me to do some things for me." Bardwick writes that middle-aged women come to understand what they must do in order to get where they want to go. Women can say: "What I have to do is what I have not done."

Like men, women confront the question of meaning in life, and they also must deal with issues of values, achievement, and personal relationships. Career women will re-evaluate work in terms of its meaning for them and for affirmation of the self. Many women construct a new role in midlife by entering the work force for the first time, or by re-entering a career temporarily given up because of family responsibilities. Others go back to school or take on responsibilities in the community.

The marital relationship is an issue for women as they search for satisfying ways to live the rest of their life. Some toy with the

idea of divorce; some go through with it. Others discover that
their husband wants out of the marriage.

**Alice Ray, aged 47, is alone and scared. After twenty-five years of
marriage and housekeeping she has just been through a traumatic
divorce. She has little money and realizes that she must get a job. She
has limited work experience outside the home and no education beyond high school. Her self-esteem is shaken, and she has only vague
ideas about how to find a job. The transition from housewife to work
may prove difficult.**

Planning for Change

Many adults will change careers four or five times during their
lifetime. The reasons most often cited for this condition are technology and changes in the economy. In the past, workers at the
lower end of the educational and socio-economic ladder were
most directly affected by changes in the labor market. But in today's economy, many experienced workers at all levels are finding themselves unemployed, and many have problems finding
another job. In order to deal with this problem J. C. Crystal and
R. N. Bolles have developed a *life-work planning* sequence applicable for the middle years:

1. Develop a "work autobiography" by reviewing all that has
been accomplished so far.
2. Identify demonstrated talents.
3. Group talents into clusters.
4. Rank the clusters from *most* to *least* preferred.
5. Identify the most important thing in your life (work, family,
leisure, etc.).
6. Identify long-range goals and possible ways to implement
them.
7. Set some immediate objectives.

Personality and situational factors influence career planning
and career change at any age. Crystal and Bolles's suggestions
account for these factors as well.

Love and Marriage

Marriage in middle age is discussed fully in chapter 5, but a few brief comments on love and marriage are necessary before leaving this chapter. Traditional marriage is the usual relationship for meeting the needs for love during adult life, but obviously, meaningful love relationships are not confined to a marriage. Marriage is the usual state for the vast majority of people, and in spite of some claims, there is good reason to believe that it is a state desired by most adults of all ages. Rubin has summarized research data on divorce and marriages in the United States. She found that more than three-fourths of the population between the ages of 20 and 64 are married. In 85 percent of all families a husband and wife live together. In seven out of eight of those husband-wife families, the husband is still in his first marriage.

Finally, as midlife men and women begin to re-examine their lives they come face to face with choices made in young adulthood. A critical analysis of love and work decisions can be threatening not only to the individual but to significant others. This re-examination is a normal developmental event that may lead to change, but it is not a crisis.

During middle age there is an increasing need for a clearer self-definition and a better understanding of the purpose of life. Midlife men and women strive for authenticity, not only in terms of who they are, but in what they do.

In our literature on middle age we tend to focus too heavily on the negative and too lightly on the positive. In love and work we are prone to accept the myth that we peak at midlife and go downhill thereafter. Nonsense! The conditions required for leading a full life are more available after 40 than during young adulthood. Middle-aged people have more control over their lives, more experience in coping, and more awareness of their own capacities than younger people. Self-fulfillment through satisfying work and intimate relationships can be an exhilarating experience for midlife people. Those who are able to love and work will find not only an emotional anchor in the middle period of life, but they can move forward with a sense of purpose for the future.

Chapter 5

Marriage and Family Relationships

Two people do not have to agree on everything
     to be together
They just have to want to be together.
If that sounds simple, try it sometime.

Paul Williams

During young adulthood most men and women find a marriage partner and enter a relationship that determines, to some extent, the future direction of their lives. The marital relationship provides us with a fortress of security, and it is our route into the adult world. The popular view in earlier days was that one took the vows, made a binding commitment to another person, and "lived happily ever after." We know now, however, that few marriages are so static; people grow and change, and the relationship may change dramatically over time. Evelyn Berger, a family issues writer, has noted that "marriage is always unfinished business." The insightful psychologist and teacher Sidney Jourard wrote that in his lifetime he had experienced several marriages—to the same woman. Jourard explained that each stage of human growth contains unique personal needs, and that the enduring marriage changes to meet those needs. He believed that greater understanding and more caring could develop during the middle years if both husband and wife remained alert to the other's needs and were willing to talk about any problem or conflict.

Several marriage and family experts view marriage as a series of developmental stages. Each stage has special tasks that must be achieved and issues that must be resolved.

The early stages are a time for exploration and examination of close relationships—a time for adjusting expectations about marriage and about life with another person. It is a period for building intimacy in the Eriksonian sense as well as for exploring possible lifestyles. S. L. Rhodes states that during the first stage of marriage a major developmental task is *intimacy vs. idealization or disillusionment.* She believes that the future of the marriage depends heavily upon the relationships developed during this period. A critical issue during this stage is dealing with reality.

Not all married couples have children, but those who do face a number of additional tasks that alter both the marital role and the couple relationship. Children require care and nurturance, decreasing the time the couple have for their own activities and for each other. During the same period, men and women are busily involved in their careers and in working to achieve personal security and financial independence. It is not surprising that marital unhappiness and divorce increases during this period. Rhodes believes that there are two major reasons for marital discord during the child-rearing years: (1) the mother-child bond may become so strong that the father feels neglected, and (2) the mother may devote so much time trying to meet the needs of a husband and children that her own needs go unmet. She states that mutual planning and open communication between husband and wife are essential if these problems are to be avoided.

It is inevitable that both men and women will change during this active period of life. Unfortunately the change often occurs without each other's awareness. Thus, two people grow apart, pursuing individual interests down separate paths. They arrive at middle age and discover that they have little in common.

The Post-Parental Years

The *post-parental years*—usually after 45—come at a time when children are grown up, forming their own friendships and striving for independence. Interaction between the couple shifts from parent-child to husband-wife: two adults again relating to each other.

This period may require some reorganization, focusing on how two adults will live together after many years of living with one or more children. Couples who have related to each other through children, or who have used a child as a buffer to minimize or avoid conflict, may find that some drastic changes in communication are necessary. Now they are on their own and must rely on their own skills in interpersonal relationships.

For many people, this post-parental period is one of the happiest in their married life. There is an initial readjustment to living without children, but after a short time many couples report heightened feelings of freedom, greater spontaneity, and more intimacy than they have experienced in years. Several studies have found that marital satisfaction increases during the post-parental years. There are some issues that must be resolved, however, and as they enter a new stage as a couple, both men and women often find a need to make substantive modifications in several components of their lives.

Levinson believes that men in their early forties begin a new period of life structure–changing during which they must accomplish three major tasks. They must terminate the period of early adulthood, take the first steps into midlife, and deal with the polarities or conflicts in their life. Levinson reports that many men begin the process of "de-illusionment" around age 40: they begin to lose or reduce the illusions of youth and early adulthood in an appropriate yet sometimes painful fashion. Levinson agrees with Jung that this is the period in life when adults begin the process of *individuation*—developing a clearer understanding between oneself and the external world.

During this transition the man may reappraise the nature of the dream he developed during young adulthood. He may wish to re-work his views of success, status, and power. In terms of career achievements, some men change the focus of their earlier ambitions and aspirations. But it may be difficult to give up one's dreams if earlier goals have not been achieved. Some men may become preoccupied with "making it," and devote even more time to the career. Marriages may suffer, and these men may develop physical and mental health problems. Ironically, the man who is so desperate in his efforts to achieve success may have greater need for a close relationship than ever before. Lowenthal feels that close interpersonal relationships serve as a resource against stress and life's crises. Much of a man's effort to achieve success, to leave something of himself behind, may be at the unconscious level; nevertheless, it can lead to misunderstanding in the husband-wife relationship and conflict in the marriage.

During the past few years a great deal has been written on midlife women, and it is now possible to discuss their reactions to this phase of the life cycle. F. B. Livson stated that "middle age can loosen the boundaries of a woman's life" and call forth suppressed parts of the self. She feels that emerging independence is the reward for a middle-aged woman. The home and family no longer dominate her time, and she is able to look to the outside world for new modes of expression.

Golan, who has written extensively about life transitions, pointed out that after her children grow up the middle-aged woman may enter or return to college or the work world, or become active in community affairs. She may engage in an extramarital affair, often in response to her husband's lack of interest and "a need to reaffirm her own sense of desirability." On the whole, most women seem able to ward off "the acute sense of crisis that some husbands may be suffering." Some researchers suggest that the issues women face during this period may lead to renewed psychological growth, because the woman responds actively, developing new interests and skills.

Mayer also believes that middle age brings new opportunities for women. She claims that women over 40 now leave home to travel, lecture, find jobs, or simply to be alone. Women are now "doing their own thing," according to Mayer. They are leaving their husbands because they are unhappy, want their freedom, or no longer wish to be married. And, they are doing so "in spite of their experiences as wage earners and without a man waiting in the wings."

Joan freed herself from the myth that a woman needs a man

to protect her. She described her feelings to a women's support group:

I resented it. I never accepted the notion that I could not do what I wanted. Traditional social dictates about the role of women are wrong. When my children were grown I decided there were other parts of life I wanted to explore. I wanted a life of my own. I had fantasies about turning back the clock, traveling across the country, and running around with a lot of men. Last year I spent a lot of time doing whatever I wanted, talking with people, visiting friends, and taking some classes at the University. We had some problems because Arthur (husband) was not always sure what was going on and sometimes he didn't know if I wanted a separation or if I was going to hang around. But we talked about our feelings and we have decided to stick with the marriage. I now know more about myself, and I feel more independent, more like a person, than I have ever felt in my life.

Many middle-aged women in this society grew up in a system of cultural arrangements that made them dependent upon men. The woman was a nest builder, a bearer of children, a nurturer of the young. Men were the protectors of women. To get a protector required getting married. To find a husband women were required to be dependent, or helpless: men were attracted to helpless women, provided they were beautiful.

There was a lot of myth and a little truth in all this—and both men and women were disadvantaged by it. They are now challenging the myth. Few women of any age want to be little girls, and most men probably prefer a companion and helpmate to a dependent, compliant wife.

The same myth that made the woman's primary role a nest builder and bearer of children carried with it the assumption that the post-parental years—the empty-nest syndrome, some called it—brought many women into a state of sadness and depression. Grief and mourning followed the departure of children; women had trouble finding meaning in life without their children. But Rubin's study of women aged 35 to 54 illustrates that, in spite of cultural practices, not all middle-aged women accept motherhood and housewifery as their primary tasks. One 43 year old interviewed by Rubin expressed her feelings about grown-up children:

Lonesome? God no! From the day the kids are born if it's not one thing it's another. After all these years of being responsible for them, you finally get to the point where you want to scream: "Fall out of the nest already, you guys, will you? It's time."

Growing Children

Young parents live with the illusion that their children will always be with them. As the woman in the above example stated, "from the day they are born," they are always around, and the parent's life is intricately tied up with the tasks, the joys, and the frustrations of parenting. We are not always certain whether our child-rearing practices are correct, and we worry about whether we are helping our children grow in the right direction. We exercise control over our children because we wish to protect them and because we feel that control and power are necessary for proper guidance and upbringing.

As we approach 40 or 45, however, and watch our children become adolescents, it becomes clear that our relationships with them are changing. They are now driving cars, dating, and going through their own transitions. We are no longer the primary persons in their lives, and we may have lost much of our power over them. Sometimes we confront them; they disagree, become moody, and think we are out of date—old fashioned, a little odd. We know that changes are taking place; we understand that the rite of passage which our children are now facing is all part of the life cycle. But we are a little apprehensive about what is happening, and a little sad that the family is no longer intact. Our children will not always be with us.

They will go on to form new families, and we will retain our emotional ties with them. We will still be a major influence in their lives, and when they have had time to become autonomous adults, they may turn to us for advice. But they are their own men and women, and we can never be certain whether we have shaped their character and personality or whether they are the products of their own minds. Erikson argues that mature midlife men and women understand that they now live between two generations—their children and their aging parents. This, too, is a normal state in the human life cycle.

Elderly Parents

Today's middle-aged people are in a unique position; they are expected to be responsive to their children and to their parents. In earlier times middle-aged people were likely to be the oldest generation, but that condition has changed dramatically. Population statistics in 1980 revealed that there were 24.4 million people aged 65 or above—more than 11 percent of the U.S. population. Moreover, the percentage of people over 85 continues to increase. Having at least one elderly parent who will require care is an increasing probability for middle-aged adults.

The importance of family contacts for the elderly has not declined in modern society, nor has physical distance and mobility separated older parents from their children. A 1982 report by Elizabeth Johnson and Donald Spence revealed that three out of four older persons with children lived in the same household as their child or within a half hour's distance of at least one child. So, contrary to popular belief, the immediate family is the major source of contact for the older person. Middle-aged children are the major caregivers for the frail older person in the United States. But caregiving for the elderly may create stress in many families. Patricia Archbold writes that families provide care for their ill elderly members at considerable hardship to the family unit. People who assume parent-caring duties do so with little social and economic support. Less than 1 percent of the budgets of Medicare and Medicaid are spent on home health services. Moreover, the social restrictions and privacy limitations imposed on those who care for the chronically ill are severe.

Middle-aged sons and daughters generally play different roles in caregiving, with men providing the financial support and women more directly involved in the day-to-day caring for the elderly person. Sometimes the tasks of caring for an elderly parent become overwhelming. One 52-year-old parent caregiver with a working husband and a teenager at home described her day:

I get up at 6:30, shower, and make coffee for my husband. He makes his own breakfast, and Rudy (son) gulps a glass of milk and they're off. I get mother up at 7:45, help her shower, then make her breakfast. She moves and eats quite slowly so by now it is 10 o'clock. I get her into the family room and turn on the TV; then I make beds and clean the house. I prepare her lunch at 12:30, then I shop and take care of other household duties while she has a nap. I begin preparing dinner at 5. Mother has trouble eating so I make special meals for her. I help her to the bathroom at 8 and get her ready for bed. After that I spend some time with Travis (husband) and read a little. By 10 I'm wiped out.

Caring for an elderly parent is not only physically demanding, but it is psychologically trying as well. Elderly people, like everyone else, have complex emotional needs, and they often expect these needs to be met by the middle-aged child. We are only beginning to understand the intricacies of the emotional relationship between adult children and aged parents, but we know that for many people it is difficult to manage. Tensions often develop in spite of serious and concentrated effort on the part of both the child and the parent. The adult child often walks a fine line between the role of helper, confidant, and nurse, and the role of a child. Many parents hang on to their power, giving orders and advice even as they are being tucked into bed by a 50-year-old child who is already a grandparent. "Don't tell me what to do, I'm your mother (or father)." Or, "you ought to. . . ."

The child may get angry and "talk back"—then feel guilty later. Or we feel angry because we think being a dutiful son (or daughter) is not enough—our efforts are not appreciated. We allow our parents some power over us, but most of us have our limits. Anger and guilt are normal feelings, and in time these feelings generally dissipate.

Most frail adults detest being unable to take care of themselves and most do not accept their dependency. They need to maintain some dignity and some control, and these efforts often lead to conflict.

Caregiving children often experience conflicts in their marital and other relationsips. The time and energy required to care for an aged relative exact a toll that is felt by the spouse and other family members. Caregiving children often feel torn between their wish to relate to the spouse as before and their desire to meet the needs of a parent. During crisis periods the marital relationship may suffer significantly. However, as Archbold stated, while some periods may be quite stressful, couples with strong relationships are usually able to manage the difficulty and later to see the situation as a growth experience. "When you go through hard times together, you grow stronger."

The death of a parent is discussed briefly in chapter 7. Here it is sufficient to say that pain and mourning, lasting for a year or more, are a quite normal reaction to the death of someone so close to us. Remembering, longing, and experiencing deep, intense feelings of sadness and guilt are among some of the usual reactions to death and loss. We each have our own way of mourning, but regardless of the form it takes, after the death of a parent the world becomes a different place. It may become empty, lonely, and harsh. Gradually, however, stability returns and we are able to get on with our lives.

McGill wrote that the death of a parent brings into clear focus the ultimate reality of one's own death. When we lose a parent we realize that immortality is an illusion and that we cannot live forever. We feel more vulnerable than we have ever felt in our lives; we could not protect our parent from death, and we cannot protect ourselves. For middle-aged men and women, this realization comes at a time when other insights are emerging, making midlife a time for re-awakening: thus it can also be a time for new opportunities and new beginnings. These happenings enable us to "see clearly now": we are more aware of what has happened and of what may happen in the future. The passing of years has brought several rewards in the form of psychological growth and keener wisdom, and we are now ready to deal with tasks that we would not touch before.

Changes in Marital Relationships

Marriage during middle age is not merely an extension of marriage during young adulthood. It is usually a longer period with unique characteristics.

Several of the circumstances of midlife marriage were identified earlier in this chapter. Changes after 40 which have implications for marital relationships were noted, but it is not just the relationship and conditions that change: midlife brings some significant changes in marriage partners themselves.

Neugarten and others have found that individuals exhibit some personality change over time, but Paul Costa and Robert McCrae wrote that most people reveal considerable continuity in personality and behavior over the life span. Several studies indicate that changes tend to be gradual—minimal in some people, dramatic in others. Moreover, the changes emerge early in some individuals, and in the later years in others.

The research on middle age—generally covering the years from the late thirties to early sixties—reveals significant and sex-related changes in both men and women over time. Personal stock-taking during the middle years often results in a revision of goals and values. Both men and women begin to look beyond work and in the direction of greater personal commitments, and women turn to new forms of achievement and expression. Orville Brim, Schlossberg, and others believe that men tend to become more interested in personal fulfillment and life satisfaction during this period, while women at midlife tend to become more assertive and aggressive. The diverging directions that men and women take may put a severe strain on the marital relationship.

Gould suggests that personality changes in middle-aged men include a reduced concern for mastery and power, and Lowenthal writes that men in their late forties and fifties become more mellow and reflective. By the mid fifties many men appear to have resolved the stresses of life and no longer focus major attention on work and success. They become more affiliative, more contented, and more concerned about making a satisfying life for themselves and their wives.

By contrast, middle-aged women become more dominant and more managerial. Neugarten found that middle-aged women began to branch out and add new roles to the traditional roles of wife and mother. The middle years represent a new period of freedom for women, a time for personal growth and for the development of creative talents. Consequently, women may focus away from the family at the very time the husband turns toward the family with renewed interest.

Margaret Zube believes that moving out, exploring new opportunities, and trying new activities can be stressful for anyone. This is particularly so for women who have no background and

MARRIAGE DECLINES

More people in their early thirties are remaining single, according to the U.S. Census Bureau.

In 1970, approximately 6 percent of women and 9 percent of men aged 30 to 34 had never married. By 1982 this figure was almost double, with 12 percent of women and 17 percent of men never married, the bureau reported.

A similar trend was found among people in their mid to late twenties. More than 20 percent of the women and almost 35 percent of the men in that age group have never married.

These changes, and a declining birth rate, have brought some major changes in Americans' living arrangements. More people now live alone or with non-relatives. The average size of an American household has declined from 3.14 persons in 1970 to 2.72 in 1982.

Reports from France reveal that marriage appears to be on the decline there also. Couples in that country appear to be "living in sin" in far greater numbers than in most places in the world. The church continually warns people that living together without benefit of clergy is breaking a taboo, but this injunction is widely ignored.

One of the factors undermining marriage in France is fiscal. Unwed people pay lower taxes than those who are married. One couple, middle aged and the parents of four teenagers, stated that they could not afford to get married.

no previous experiences for exploring possibilities for a career or for the development of creative talents. Husbands who do not understand their wives' outward movement may become confused and frustrated; wives may resent the husband's increased demands on their time. Some marriage counselors feel that these are among the most stressful elements in midlife marriages.

Many midlife women, of course, do not move outward for new careers or new activities. They find fulfillment within the family and continue to play a dominant role with their husband and grown children. They report increased satisfaction with life and ascribe their happiness to their family as well as to their own activities.

There is growing evidence that married couples develop unique patterns of interaction and intimacy in the first few years of marriage and that the stresses noted in midlife marital relationships are actually lifelong differences. The differences take on greater significance during the middle years when events of that period lead to personal stock-taking and evaluation. Lowenthal feels that middle-aged and older people are more open about problems in relationships and thus more likely to report them.

Satisfying marriage relationships appear to contribute to happiness and well-being throughout life. (But marriages that are lasting are not necessarily those which are most satisfying.) B. C. Rollins and H. Feldman, authorities on marriage and family, report that marital satisfaction generally shows a progressive decline from the time children are born through middle age, with an upswing after that. Stress, associated with the numerous tasks of child-rearing, work, and financial pressures, are among the most common factors in marital discord among young adults. As children grow up, most couples report new freedom and a different form of a couple relationship: calmer, more objective, and more secure.

Midlife maturity, contrary to some of the literature, does not diminish passion and sexual intimacy. Researchers at the University of Southern California report that sexual intimacy is "equally important for young and middle-aged lovers." The implication is that in satisfying relationships, passion maintains its importance in love through middle age. Several other factors contribute to marital happiness and sustain the relationship through the years. George Levinger reported that loyalty, similarity, commitment, and security are important factors in married relationships during all ages.

Separation, Divorce, and Remarriage

Midlife is a time for resolution: we question the decisions made in our twenties and attempt to correct some of the problems and misunderstandings that now interfere with our lives. During this period some couples discover serious problems in the marriage, and one or both of the partners may decide that there is little basis for a relationship. Separation or divorce may provide a release—a chance to start over at midlife.

Movies, television, and best-selling novels depict divorce as a normal life event, contributing to the belief that it may happen to any of us. The 1980 census data suggests that the divorce rate continues relatively high, but across all age groups it has slowed from approximately 8 percent annually in the 1960s to 4 percent in 1980. Divorce is more likely during the early years of marriage. U.S. Census Bureau figures from 1976–77 show that almost two-thirds of all women whose first marriage ended in divorce were divorced before age 30. Some studies have found that the divorce rate among couples aged 30 and under exceeds 15 percent annually.

After 30, the fever appears to subside, for a few years at least. Marriages become more stable and breakups fall below 7 percent annually. But the statistics climb again in the 40 to 45 age group, and the percentage of people separated and divorced reaches 10 percent. After 55 divorce occurs less frequently, and it is rare after age 70.

Divorce rates in the United States reflect a range of social patterns. College graduates and persons with a good income are less likely to divorce. The divorce rate is higher among black persons. The percentage of divorced and not remarried is higher for women than men.

Just as marriage involves a major life transition—role change and status change—so does divorce. But unlike marriage, the roles for divorced men and women are not socially prescribed; there are no guidelines for starting over, particularly at middle age. These conditions contribute to some of the fear and emotional upset generally associated with divorce. For middle-aged men and women, divorce means, among other things, a change in social relationships and a change in economic status. Some middle-aged couples go from a relatively comfortable life to one of financial hardship and deprivation. One 50-year-old woman explained her plight:

What am I supposed to do? I was married for twenty-nine years and all of a sudden he left me. Moved in with a woman younger than his daughter! He had an income of almost $50,000 a year and we had a good life. Now I have no job and a house I can't keep up the payments on. So, I'll sell the house and go back to school. If I can become a nurse maybe I can find work. Now, who wants to hire a 50-year-old woman?

The process of separation and divorce can lead to enormous stress for both partners. David Chiriboga studied more than 300 men and women who had filed for divorce in California. He concluded that the process was often traumatic, generally more so than the troubles associated with the marriage. Shifting gears from marriage to singlehood was quite difficult and created a demand for new learning, and relearning of appropriate behaviors. Chiriboga believes that the stresses of separation are often more difficult for men than for women. He suggests this problem may stem from the tendency of American men to deny or suppress the existence of personal problems.

Forming new attachments can be awkward and frightening. There are no rules for "once married," over-40 singles. In her best-selling novel *Second Heaven*, Judith Guest describes how her central character, Michael, tried to learn "how to have fun" again. Michael, middle aged and divorced, decided he would go to parties, tell jokes, get drunk, meet some nice woman, take her to bed, and exchange phone numbers the next morning. He did that a few times, and he also hung around bars where people went to make plans for the weekend. But he could never get the hang of it. He decided he was too old to sit in bars with a silly grin on his face waiting for something to happen.

The divorced person's life does not remain stressed and disoriented. Gradually, the person begins to restore order to her or his life and to function as an autonomous individual. Most divorced persons eventually remarry. U.S. Census Bureau reports show that three out of four women and five out of six men who are divorced will eventually remarry. The data is not conclusive on this point, but there are some indications that second marriages have a slightly better survival rate than the first.

Divorce at midlife is not necessarily an emotionally charged experience. Divorce can result from the recognition that there is little reason to continue the marriage. Some couples recognize that they have grown apart, and they are able to end a relationship without bitterness. They have a few years of a shared past, but no real basis for a future. Divorce will permit them to pursue new interests and new directions as they enter the second half of the life cycle.

Earl and Darcy Bolton graduated from the same Midwestern high school at 18. Married a year later, their only child, a daughter, Alexandria, was born when they were 21. Soon thereafter, the Boltons moved East where Earl had a job with a distant relative, a plumbing contractor. Over the next few years Earl became quite successful as a plumber and later as a sub-contractor. He built an expensive house, participated in civic affairs, and became a respected leader in the community. Darcy was active on the library board and a member of the church choir.

By age 40 Earl and Darcy had established a stable life structure, but soon thereafter Earl began to feel unhappy, trapped in decisions made in early adulthood. The job became boring, and he began to feel out of touch with Darcy and their daughter. He grew moody and lonely and according to his own statements "brooded about my health and worried about death." Within a few months he was being treated for an ulcer. He went through a tormenting reappraisal of his marriage, and Darcy agreed to a trial separation. This arrangement lasted for three months; Darcy began dating a widowed teacher and asked Earl for a divorce. After twenty-three years of marriage they agreed to a property settlement and were granted what Earl called an "amicable divorce." They remain on friendly terms. Darcy is considering remarriage, and Earl is beginning to succeed in making his life different from what it was as a young adult.

The timing of our lives is quite different from that of our grandparents. Education lasts longer, the childbearing period is shorter, families are smaller, and medical science has increased adult life expectancy. Most adults have considerably more retirement time, and more time for mature relationships. Trends in marriage and family relationships reflect patterns of change in American society.

While there are several kinds of marriages in contemporary culture—including cohabitation, open marriage, group marriage, and homosexual marriage—90 percent of all married people in this country are in a traditional relationship. Married people are generally happier than unmarried people and have a longer life expectancy than those who remain single. People who have been married once and who have lost a spouse as a result of death or divorce tend to remarry. Men tend to remarry more often than women. Second marriages, particularly in middle age and later life, appear to be more successful than first marriages. Middle-aged persons tend to have a "live and let live" attitude toward the spouse and are less likely to find fault with their partner.

Age is becoming less of a factor in selecting a mate. There are undoubtedly more "May-September" and "May-December" marriages now than in our grandparents' day. Still, the average difference in age between a man and woman is about 3.5 years for first marriages. The difference increases to 6 years in after-age-35 marriages, with the man generally older. But the range increases as much as twenty-five years when people marry after age 50: again, it is most often the male who is older.

Defining marital satisfaction is risky. Generally, it depends on who makes the judgment. Several experts believe that the major ingredients for a happy marriage include: commitment to the partner and the relationship, intimacy, openness and honesty, and being the other's primary person.

Chapter 6

Life Events and Transitions

To every thing there is a season, and a time to every
purpose under the heaven;
A time to be born, and a time to die;
A time to plant, and a time to pluck up that which is
planted;
A time to kill, and a time to heal;
A time to break down, and a time to build up;
A time to weep, and a time to laugh;
A time to mourn, and a time to dance;
A time to cast away stones, and a time to gather stones
together;
A time to embrace, and a time to refrain from
embracing;
A time to seek, and a time to lose;
A time to keep, and a time to cast away;
A time to mend, and a time to sew;
A time to keep silence, and a time to speak;
A time to love, and a time to hate;
A time for war, and a time for peace.

Ecclesiastes

On the journey across the life span we encounter a myriad of events that may change its direction. Many life events are followed by a period of transition as the person adapts to a new role or a new task. The concept of life events and transitions was introduced in chapter 1. Here this concept is used as a framework for further exploration of midlife behavior.

At age 40, 50, or 60, if we stop and consider the thousands of events—large and small—that have punctuated our lives, we have some notion of how powerful these events have been. Consider, for example, such events as entering school, our first love affair, or finding a job. Each of these events can probably be understood as important antecedents of behavior, influencing development over the life course.

Some life events can be described as internal, caused by normal growth, as in the case of puberty. Others are cultural or social, such as employment or a geographical relocation. Some events are customary—that is, they happen to most people in a given society; they are regulated, to some degree, and may be age-related. Some examples of customary events are graduation, marriage, and retirement. Life is also marked by events that are noncustomary, unregulated, and unusual, including severe illness, inheriting a fortune, or losing a job. Still others such as war, earthquake, or economic depression are political or physical events beyond the control of most individuals, but nevertheless they have an impact on large numbers of people. Economic depression is a widely used illustration of how a national or worldwide event changes millions of lives.

Major Events of Adult Life

Some major events have a high correlation with age. Neugarten believes that across the life span some events are "on time" and others are "off time." She points out that from birth to death we pass through a series of socially regulated age statuses. There is a timetable for major events: becoming independent, entering the world of work, and bearing children. Men and women are aware of how the social time clock operates and conscious of the timing of events in their own lives, describing themselves as early, late, or on time regarding school, marriage, their first job, and so on.

Neugarten wrote that on-time events are usually not upsetting; they are anticipated and rehearsed. But the unanticipated, off-time event may be shattering. According to Neugarten, "major stresses are caused by events that upset the rhythm and sequence of the life cycle." When the death of a parent comes in adolescence rather than in middle age; when the birth of a child is too early or too late; when occupational achievement is delayed; and when retirement, major illness, or widowhood occur off schedule, the event is likely to be seen as traumatic.

Most people, thinking of the future and of all the events that occur across the life span, often ponder such questions as: "Will that happen to me?" "When will it happen?" "What will it be like?" While the correlation between chronological age and some events is clear, individual variability is great. Further, there will be a wide range of reactions to the various events, and obviously many remain beyond our control. Tables 1 and 2 give some examples of major events across the adult life span and in middle age.

Table 1. Customary and Noncustomary Events of Adult Life

Customary	Noncustomary
(*High Probability of Occurrence*)	(*Low Probability of Occurrence*)
Completing Education	Serving in Military
Getting First Job	Losing Job—Being Fired
Marrying	Divorcing—Remarrying
Becoming a Parent	Suffering Severe Illness/Incapacitation
Having Children in School	Experiencing Death of a Child
Buying First Home	Winning a Lottery
Moving (Geographic)	Experiencing Earthquake, War, or
Being Promoted	Plague
Retiring	Running for Governor
Starting Second Career	Having Sex Change Operation

Table 2. Some Customary Events of Midlife

(*High Probability of Occurrence*)

Departure of Children	Death of a Parent
Promotion	Menopause (Women)
Geographic Move	Decline in Testosterone (Men)
Attainment of Financial Security	Children's Marriages
"Topping Out" in Career	Extramarital Affair

Henry Gee, aged 42, asked for counseling on a number of problems that had been "piling up lately." After twenty years of marriage, his wife, Ellen, aged 40, has become sullen and uncooperative and she is now beginning to drink more than Henry thinks is "good for her." They have three children: Joe, 17; Maria, 15; and Suzanne, 14. The children bicker constantly with each other and their mother.

Henry has been working two jobs for the past two years in order to "provide properly" for his family. He is their only support. Lately, he states he has not felt well, has developed ulcers, and has trouble sleeping. He has not discussed these matters with his wife, because "we rarely talk anymore."

During the past four months he has been having an affair with a younger woman.

Henry is depressed and angry. He asked for help in getting along better with his wife and dealing with their financial problems.

Henry described his life as "generally unhappy, particularly in the last three or four years." The gap between what he wanted out of life and what he was getting seemed to be growing wider. He felt trapped—angry with present conditions and uncertain about the future.

Brim has identified the relationship between events and social roles. Marriage, starting a home, and becoming a parent are all events and activities that are related to social life. Havighurst describes the link between age, events, and developmental tasks. He believes that the primary tasks of middle age include: assisting teen-age children to become responsible adults, achieving social and civic responsibility, reaching and maintaining satisfactory performance in one's career, developing leisure activities, relating to one's spouse as a person, and adjusting to aging parents.

David Hulstch and J. K. Plemons discuss gains and losses associated with life events. In middle age, achieving the financial security necessary to be one's own person could be considered a gain, whereas losing a job would be a loss. Put another way, some events are negative and some are positive; some are desired, and others are quite undesired.

In the view of several psychologists life events are noteworthy, primarily because they require a change of behavior on the part of the person who experiences them. Getting a promotion to a new job with more status and greater financial rewards will undoubtedly change one's behavior as well as one's view of the self.

Some events may have both pleasant and unpleasant consequences. A promotion is generally viewed as a pleasant event—but if it requires a move across the country, leaving friends and acquaintances, it can also bring unpleasant or negative results. Inheriting a fortune may thus be the most pleasant route to affluence. While this latter event may require the recipient to purchase a parking meter at the local Internal Revenue Service office, at least he or she is spared the major hassle of moving. The point here is that the most significant life events lead to behavior change—they require some adjustments in living, sometimes temporarily, and sometimes for the remainder of one's life.

The period of adapting or changing to meet the conditions is often referred to as the *transition*—though some authorities use *event, transition,* and *change* as synonyms. Sometimes the term *transition* is used to describe the passage from a stable state to a state of uncertainty on the way to a new stable state. The transition may involve limited change in one's style of living, or it may require major change and readjustment. For example, when the last child leaves home and starts a separate life, some parents may experience only a limited change in their life. But if the parents have decided to sell the house and move to a small, more economical apartment across town, the change may require a major reorganization of their living habits. The effects may be transitory and perhaps pleasant, but they require a period of transition that is sometimes marked by feelings of anxiety and insecurity.

Life Events and Stress

All life events are potentially stressful, to the extent that they produce anxiety or require change in a person's life. This means that even pleasant events (getting married, winning a lottery) may be stressful, just as unpleasant events (getting fired, getting a speeding ticket) are. Stress can be broadly defined as the physical or psychological reaction to the event. Stress or crisis does not

Rank	Event	Life Change Unit (Weight)
1	death of spouse	100
2	divorce	73
3	marital separation	65
4	jail term	63
5	death of close family member	63
6	personal injury or illness	53
7	marriage	50
8	fired at work	47
9	marital reconciliation	45
10	retirement	45
11	change in health of family member	44
12	pregnancy	40
13	sex difficulties	39
14	gain of new family member	39
15	business readjustment	39
16	change in financial state	38
17	death of close friend	37
18	change to different line of work	36
19	change in number of arguments with spouse	35
20	mortgage over $10,000	31
21	foreclosure of mortgage or loan	30
22	change in responsibilities at work	29
23	son or daughter leaving home	29
24	trouble with in-laws	29
25	outstanding personal achievement	28
26	wife begins or stops work	26
27	begin or end school	26
28	change in living conditions	25
29	revision of personal habits	24
30	trouble with boss	23
31	change in work hours or conditions	20
32	change in residence	20
33	change in schools	20
34	change in recreation	19
35	change in church activities	19
36	change in social activities	18
37	mortgage or loan less than $10,000	17

Rank	Event	Life Change Unit (*Weight*)
38	change in sleeping habits	16
39	change in number of family get-togethers	15
40	change in eating habits	15
41	vacation	13
42	Christmas	11
43	minor violations of the law	11

come from the event itself, but rather from the person's reaction to the event.

J. Holmes and S. Rahe developed the *Social Readjustment Rating Scale* to measure the amount of stress for several life events, listing events and giving a weight to each.

According to Holmes and Rahe there is a close relationship between the total number of life change units and physical or psychological illness. The greater the number of life change units the greater likelihood that illness will result. Hans Selye, an internationally acclaimed scientist, supports the Holmes and Rahe conclusions on the negative effects of stress. Selye claims that "mental tension, frustrations, insecurity, and aimlessness" are among the most damaging stressors. They cause headaches, ulcers, heart attacks, suicide, or just plain unhappiness.

Stress and Personality Types

There are several indications that our personality controls our vulnerability to stress. Individual reactions to an event vary considerably. Arguments with a spouse may be viewed as quite normal and devoid of stress by one person. But for another individual an argument with a husband or wife may be quite stressful. Some researchers have studied personality types and the incidence of coronary disease in men. M. Friedman and R. H. Rosenman identified two personality types, A and B. The type A person tended to respond to everyday situations in such a way that stress became an aspect of daily living. He was highly competitive, hard-driving, impatient, and always in a hurry. The type

A men were quick to anger, aggressive, often tense, and engaged in few recreational activities. The type B men were less aggressive, more relaxed, slow to anger, happier, and less competitive. Friedman and Roseman reported that type A men were more likely to have heart attacks than type B, and five times more likely to suffer a second heart attack. Personality type was especially useful as a predictor of heart disease in men aged 39 to 49.

It is risky, of course, to draw sharp conclusions from this research. It is easy to find people who do not fit either the type A or the type B mold.

Alan Moore grew up in a family that scratched a living from a small farm in the foothills of the Appalachians. Alan worked on the farm during most of his childhood and adolescence and rode a school bus eleven miles to the County High School. By the time he graduated he was in rebellion against the lonely life and the hard times and decided he would leave the farm forever. He wanted to be an engineer and that is what he did. He worked his way through the university, graduating with honors two weeks before the Korean War erupted. He was an infantry officer in Korea and was twice decorated for heroism.

After the war he took a job in Washington with a marine parts manufacturing company and in two years was promoted to supervisor. He stated that he "loved the job," often working twelve hours per day even though the extra time was not required. As the company grew Alan moved up the ladder and was the chief engineer at 30 and general manager by 40.

Alan married at age 29 and almost a quarter century later his wife described him as a "kind man, quiet, and easy to live with." She said he was not a demonstrative person, but she and their two children knew he loved them.

When he was growing up, feelings were not shared, and expressions of warmth were infrequent. In Alan's view, the family members cared about each other, but found it awkward to say so.

At age 54 Alan was still a hard-working man, impatient with mediocrity and convinced "each person must have some goals, something they want to accomplish." He said he had achieved his career goals and felt satisfied with his job. He "hadn't even thought" about retirement and he had not "slowed down." He was in love with his wife and proud of their two children. The only thing he would do differently if he were starting over: "I would take several art courses."

In the fifth decade of life Alan had not spent one day of his life in a hospital and described his health as "excellent." In a discussion of his satisfaction with life he remarked: "Anyone who claims to be free of worries or problems is either a liar or a fool. Sure, I have my ups and downs. But my work has always sustained me, and having a wife like Louise, who is also my best friend, has made it all worthwhile."

Alan, by most available measures, has adapted quite well to normal life changes. He is a self-sufficient hard-driving man, reasonably happy. His family respects and admires him. For Alan, his way of life has produced few problems.

Stress and Midlife

All human beings experience stress. Over the life span, however, the stressors change character. Young adults are under pressure to "make something" of themselves, to become independent, and start a new family. We encourage young people to be hard-working, aggressive, and successful—all actions that may produce stress.

By the middle years adults are supposed to have achieved success—but we know that this is not always the case. Many people at 40 or 50 have not yet achieved success in their careers, nor are they financially independent. Many have spent years raising a family, often in a job and in an economy that is uncertain. In middle age many women enter or re-enter the work force, in an attempt to enhance the family's financial status or to assist children with educational expenses. Many people at this age feel anxious because they have not yet achieved the success that is considered normal in middle age. Some have not yet reached their personal goals; many are bored with their jobs, disillusioned with marriage, and uncertain about the future. A few will literally work themselves to death, trying to save face.

Despite these conditions, there is little evidence that midlife is more stressful than other life stages. Several major studies reveal that for many people, work and marriage are not sources of stress at all; rather, they are sources of satisfaction and security.

Coping with Stress

During World War II a Russian peasant, opposed to violence and uncertain about the future, moved his family into the deep forests of the Ural Mountains, far from any village and beyond the reach of civilization. Thirty years later, Russian engineers searching for minerals found the old peasant and one surviving son. Wrapped in animal skins and disease-ridden, the aged man and the son cringed in fear at the sight of other humans.

In the 1970s, thousands of Americans fled the cities in search of a more simple life in the rural areas of the country. They were fed up with air pollution, crime and violence, congestion, and the frustrations of big city life. They soon discovered, however, that the pastoral life also has its frustrations, often requires hard work, and can be more expensive than high-rise living. In 1984, *USA Today* reported that many of the 1970s homesteaders are eagerly returning to the city. They are frustrated by increasing costs of transportation, the absence of city conveniences, and the perils of country roads in winter.

Neither modern Americans nor Russian peasants can avoid the stress of living in a complex society. We are all at times tempted by the thought of "getting away from it all," but few of us really wish to be totally isolated from the activity and the excitement of a social environment. Selye has stated that stress is the spice of life. We can avoid stress only by doing nothing—a life that few people would enjoy. There are numerous activities in life which are stressful, but which are essential to good health. Thus, the belief that "stress kills" is inaccurate. Some people adopt self-defeating and ineffective methods of coping and in these cases stress can be harmful or even deadly.

How, then, can we avoid harmful stress?

Briefly, we can select a spouse whom we love and respect; we can choose friends whom we enjoy and like, and we can find a job that meets our self-sufficiency needs for activity, creativity, and self-esteem. Only then can we reduce the possibilities of constant stress.

How can we better cope with unavoidable stress?

Most people cope effectively with stress, even in the face of severe loss, crisis, or disappointment. Unusual demands and pressures, however, may call upon all our skills and resources, and the following suggestions may be helpful:

• Share feelings and emotions with another person—spouse, relative, or a close friend.

• Continue normal activities and responsibilities if at all possible—or resume usual activities as soon as possible.

• Avoid making major decisions until the crisis or stress period dissipates.

• Pursue some new interests or engage in some favorite activities.

• Seek professional help. If you are unable to cope with stress after a normal lapse of time, a counselor, psychologist, or psychiatrist may be helpful.

WHAT CONCERNS ADULTS?

What do we worry about? Responses to this question are elusive and shaped by world events and changing personal circumstances.

Surveys to determine what issues or problems give us cause to worry are numerous, and results are varied. The data reported here is from three surveys from 1983 and 1984 which asked as many as 1,000 adult men and women what concerned them the most. According to statistics from those surveys our biggest worries include:

> The economy
> Personal finances
> Unemployment
> Nuclear war
> Education of youth

Obviously we believe there is something to worry about. It is also interesting to note that people tended to mention those issues that affect the nation as a whole and not strictly personal concerns.

Chapter 7

Facing Death

Not to laugh, not to lament,
Not to curse, but to understand.
                                        Spinoza

It may seem strange to discuss death in a book on midlife. But death is a part of the life cycle, and awareness of death has a profound effect on the way we live, especially in middle age.

The inevitability of our own mortality becomes quite clear during the first few years of the midlife period. During this stage several internal and external events send some clear messages that the ultimate outcome of life is death. These messages come in the form of changes in our own body, grown-up children recording the passage of years, and illness and death of our friends and parents. These events break through our illusions of immortality and heighten our awareness that there is an end to life's story.

Elliott Jacques, who coined the term "midlife crisis," writes that the midpoint of life means that a person has "grown up and has begun to grow old." New questions and problems will emerge in midlife, and new strategies for coping with them must be developed. The first phase of adult life is complete; youth is over and its loss will be mourned. The major psychological task for this period is to achieve social status as a mature adult. The paradox in this period is that this achievement and fulfillment may be muted by awareness of death. Jacques believes that facing the reality of one's own death is the crucial feature of the midlife stage.

Arthur, a successful 43-year-old executive, described how he felt when confronted with the fact of mortality. "Until a few months ago I gave little thought to dying; I have been too busy living for that. Then my uncle died at 61 and that hit me, really hit me. I am at the top of the ladder now, and I wonder what it all means anyway. I hope death is a long way off, but now I know it is there, and I have a different slant on life. So, I came to you because I want to consider how I can change some things . . . how I can live a little better while I am still young."

The growing awareness of one's own inevitable death is generally viewed as a major factor in the midlife re-examination discussed in the previous chapter and illustrated in the above vignette. In some cases awareness that life does not go on forever brings on such self-destructive behaviors as alcoholism, drug abuse, and depression. Some reports suggest that there is a link between suicide and awareness of death, but this information has not been verified. In fact, Knox reports that suicide rates are considerably higher for people over 60 than for midlife adults.

Some people react to mortality by turning to religion and striving for inner peace and harmony; they may show more interest in their family and the community. Others become concerned about their health: they diet, give up smoking, and embark on physical fitness programs. Except for a general review of life, however, there is little evidence of a patterned response to the inevitability of death. In midlife when we have our first major confrontation with our own mortality we may have some deep thoughts about death; we may feel sad, and we probably dread it. But there is little evidence that we are terrorized by the knowledge that death waits ahead.

Dying in Contemporary Society

Social attitudes and customs affect the way we react to death and the acceptance of our personal mortality. Death is not an individual act any more than life is. Philippe Aries writes that, like every other milestone in life, death is celebrated by a ceremony that is more or less solemn and whose purpose is to express the individual's solidarity with the family and community.

Present attitudes about death are quite different from prevailing attitudes through much of history. The ancient Greeks, for example, faced death as they faced life—openly and directly. To live fully and die gloriously was a prevalent aspiration among the Greeks. Up through the Middle Ages, when life expectancy was short and before modern medicine offered some protection against early and untimely death, people were more aware of death and of the process of dying.

Barbara Tuchman, in her history of the Middle Ages, vividly describes reactions to the deadly plagues of the fourteenth century. This dreaded scourge claimed old and young, saint and sinner, prince and pauper: all bowed to this calamity of calamities. Families were wiped out in a matter of days, and communities were decimated in a season. One who survives such an ordeal will almost certainly become reconciled to death.

Kubler-Ross believes that a change of focus from the individual to the masses has influenced contemporary attitudes about death. In the old days man could look his enemy in the face and have a fighting chance in a personal encounter with a visible foe. Now we have many weapons of mass destruction. Some of these cannot be seen, and their destructive power cannot even be measured. Death comes out of the sky or in the form of chemicals and gases. It is invisible, impersonal, and lethal. Thus, a person has no defense individually—everyone is threatened and chances for survival are low.

David Dempsey suggests that we have trouble dealing with the concept of death because it violates the rule that we must be happy at all times. Thus, we try to suppress the death anxiety, and even physicians and other health-care professionals prefer to avoid the topic. For physicians, death represents a defeat of their purposes, a gap in their knowledge, and a deficit in their skills.

Aries writes that in our desire to avoid death we often conceal the truth even from people who are dying. Except for the death of public figures—statesmen and celebrities, for example—society is attempting to banish all recognition of death. This is contrary to everything that has happened in life, according to Aries. The death of any person who has participated in life affects the community. We delude ourselves when we try to go on as if no-body died anymore.

Western society attempts to avoid facing death in other ways. When people are sick and old we remove them from the community and shift them to hospitals and nursing homes. Once dead, the person is quietly and quickly removed from the premises—to be embalmed and made up to look "alive" or "natural," or perhaps to be cremated. In many cases the body of the person is never seen again.

It is obvious, then, that many people are convinced that death is something to be avoided. Brian Hall, president of the Center for Exploration of Values and Meaning, believes that we attempt to avoid death because we focus so intently upon preserving life, defining life as the absence of death. Hall contends that we are now experiencing an era that robs a dying person of the right to die and robs her or his friends of the right to mourn. He maintains that the issue of death is the consciousness of one's life and its relationship to dying. Dying is a process. According to Hall, the inability of a people or a society to cope with dying is a crisis in individuality or human identity.

Individual Reactions to Death

Some psychologists believe that death is a basic human anxiety; there is a universal fear of death that affects all aspects of life. Ernest Becker wrote that people have a terror of dying and that this terror is all-consuming when we look death in the face. According to Becker, the idea of death, the fear of it, "haunts the human animal" like nothing else; it is the mainspring of our activity—activity designed to avoid death, to overcome it by denying that death is the final destiny of man.

Death has a different meaning and impact on people during different periods of the life cycle. Lidz notes that children come to have some understanding of death by age 4 or 5. Their concerns, however, have more to do with separation from parents than with their own death. With the coming of adulthood, and particularly with marriage and parenthood, concerns about death increase. Parents may be concerned about what will happen to their children should they die and take precautions for the sake of the family as much as for themselves. We can also see how, despite strong self-preservation drives, parents stand ready to give up their lives to spare their children.

Attitudes toward death continue to change with age. The evidence suggests that once middle-aged people are through with the initial stages of awareness of personal death, their thoughts about the topic are no more frequent than those of any other age group. Furthermore, the assumption that elderly people think a lot about death is questionable. Lowenthal is in agreement with Lidz, who writes that the elderly have had several experiences with death; they know it is inevitable, and they spend little time worrying about it.

There appears to be some relationship between gender and individual reactions to death. Gould writes that men seem to be more surprised at the fact of mortality than women. They often react to news of a death as though someone has played a trick on them. Gould believes that midlife men may become quite fearful of death when friends or relatives die.

Many men see work success as a way to avoid death. According to Gould, men seem to feel they have a pact with the world: work hard, and be a good boy, and survival is assured. One of the appeals of the business world is that it has banned frailty; success can overcome any flaw, even a weakness of biology. But one success may not do it; one must keep working for a higher level in order to avoid annihilation.

After a while, of course, the pact is broken. Added responsibilities and coveted privileges offer no lasting protection against death at midlife. It is a no-win situation; sooner or later the message gets through and we realize that no matter how successful we are, we will one day die. This recognition can be a growth experience. Once we are over the initial shock and when we stop deluding ourselves, we often discover parts of ourselves that we had not noticed before.

Gerald, age 46, described what happened to him after a serious illness. "If you had asked me about life two years ago I would have

told you that I had about everything I wanted. But things changed when I lay there wondering if I was going to make it. When I realized that my life was not all I wanted it to be, I wondered what I had really accomplished and whether my presence in this world had made a difference to anybody. I realized that everything I had would fall apart or decay after I died, but more than that I came to realize that I had not been a very happy person. Well I got well, thank God, and I learned a good lesson. I'm doing some work now that will help a lot of people and that is what it is all about. Many people never learn that, but I'm glad I did because it has changed my life."

Death and the Midlife Crisis

As early adulthood comes to an end, men and women find themselves dealing more often with physiological change and a sense of aging. As noted earlier in this volume, middle-aged persons cannot run as far, play as hard, or go with as little sleep as they once could. They may be more prone to aches and pains and experience more illness, more reminders of physical deterioration and death. In these and other ways we pass from the stage of "young" to "middle aged." Individual reactions to the transition to middle age have been analyzed by several people.

Jacques believes that a midlife crisis occurs in some form in most people around age 35. This crisis is most evident in creative activities. He writes that the crisis may take three forms: the creative career may simply come to an end, either in a drying-up of creative work, or in actual death; the creative capacity may begin to show for the first time; or a decisive change in the quality and content of creativeness may take place. Jacques claims that the change in creativity during this period is found in the work of countless artists. His sample of 310 painters, composers, poets, writers, and sculptors reveals that the death rate among creative people takes a sharp jump between the age of 35 and 39. Jacques offers no explanation for the higher death rate among this group, but he does state that awareness of death brings on a crisis which in turn results in a change of direction in life.

Jacques suggests that in midlife there is a need for "self-mourning," the mourning of one's own eventual death, and for working it through one's unconscious to the point that concerns with death do not block emotional growth. In other words, a person must grow up emotionally and resolve psychological issues with death before he or she can live fully. This point of view is also found in Erikson's work. He argues that the healthy person develops a realistic view of himself and the world.

The intrusion of the reality of one's own death on the psychological scene can lead one to a resolution of conflicts and dissatisfaction in life. Ellen, aged 41, described her reaction to her mother's death:

"I looked at her lying dead and said," 'My God! She is dead, and someday I will die too, and I haven't really lived yet. I have been too busy helping other people meet their needs and I have met none of my own. My adult life has been spent mothering, wife-ing, and housekeeping. I must change that before it is too late.' It was as though I threw a brick in the air and stood under it. When I wanted to go back to college my husband couldn't accept it, so we separated. I go where I want and I have dates and live my own life. Soon I will have my degree and I will be able to do what I have wanted for years. I love it!"

Careful evaluation of several studies of midlife and close analysis of data from psychological reports reveal some paradoxical observations about awareness of death and the midlife "crisis." Jacques's report clearly charts the relationship between death, midlife, and crisis. But other reports describe the confrontation with death as a learning and liberating experience and do not speak of the anxiety and depression commonly associated with the crisis view. They describe changes in values, in life goals, and in relationships. These people do not have negative or pessimistic feelings when they consider their own death. Thus it seems unfair to suggest that awareness of one's mortality inevitably results in a crisis.

Loss and Grief

Many professionals feel that several midlife events can be viewed as losses and that the emotional reactions to any loss are genuine grief and mourning experiences. They describe the loss of youthful dreams, waning physical powers, and change in physical appearance as events that bring grief to midlife adults. Some authorities hold that divorce, at any stage of life, is consonant with many of the loss and grief experiences associated with death. This view has some support in research and in clinical experience. But here I consider only the ultimate loss: death of significant persons. Grief is the emotional suffering caused by that loss, and mourning is a process of grieving.

Midlife is the period when our parents grow old and die. Illness and death of a parent brings on a terrible sense of helplessness, loneliness, and gloom. As children we feared losing our parents, and we may have had nightmares about our loss. As adults we come to understand the reality of death and we are no longer terrorized by the thought of it, but we still dread it and have difficulty with thoughts of losing our parents.

When death does come to a parent, there may be a period of denial, a vain hope that "death can't happen now," a feeling that it is "only a dream." Soon, however, the recognition that death has occurred must be faced.

Intense grief and mourning follow. Gould writes that during the period of mourning, which may last for months or years, sequences of denial alternate with periods of grief. In denial, we try to turn the uncontrollable reality back into a dream. It is essential to bear the grief of mourning if we are to stay in touch with reality and ourselves. Clinging to the hope that death is a bad dream falsifies reality and closes off a section of our mind. The pain of longing and remembering must be endured. One cannot go on with normal life believing that death can be cheated or denied.

The death of a spouse at any stage of life comes as a cataclysmic blow. During young adulthood the death of a spouse is rare. However, between ages 40 and 60 considerably more people are widowed, mainly because of heart attacks, renal disease, and cancer. Judith Stevens-Long reports that by the mid-fifties, 52 percent of the female population and 19 percent of the male population in the United States are widowed.

Grief—intense overpowering grief—is a natural reaction to the death of someone we committed our life to. It is not, as a few have suggested, a sign of weakness or self-indulgence. The loss of intimacy, security, and closeness is difficult to describe until it is experienced. Margaret, aged 46, describes the sudden death of her 51-year-old husband:

"I couldn't believe it at first. When the hospital called and said Dave had died of a heart attack I just knew it was a mistake. Not Dave; not us. Then when I saw him at the funeral home I still couldn't accept it. I kept thinking I ought to take him home. For days I would go to the cemetery; I would talk to him and tell him to come back to me. I walked through the house at night crying and beating the walls, and more than once I was angry; no, furious, at being so alone. Then reality finally hit me and I was full of grief and terrified by the thought of going on alone."

Anger and guilt are also normal reactions to death. Erick Lindermann, a psychiatrist, studied normal grief and grouped grief symptoms into five categories: guilt, anger, preoccupation with the image of the deceased, change in conduct, and emotional distress. Many widowed people experience headaches, digestive problems, rheumatism, sleeplessness, and other stress-related disorders. Both widows and widowers report that their general health declines after the loss of the mate.

The death of a parent, a spouse, or anyone personally close and significant changes us and our world dramatically. For a time we feel intense loneliness; our life may be empty and meaningless. The world may appear drab, harsh, and cold. Some grief-stricken persons turn to others for comfort and understanding, some become involved in religion, and a few turn inward and deal with the loss in their own way.

Even as the person struggles with the grieving process, he or she is expected to react with the world and make adaptations to changes brought about by death. Golan has identified three psychosocial tasks that must be completed in the process of adapting to the death of a loved one: (1) bridging the past, (2) living with the present, and (3) finding a path into the future. Adaptation takes place gradually. Over time, perhaps months or years, we begin to find some measure of stability, and we are again able to function and to adapt to the loss.

At an adult self-help group meeting focusing on adjustment to the death of a loved one, Claire, an attractive woman in her fifties, shared her experiences with the group:

She was married to Dale for thirty-one years, and they had rarely been apart for more than a day or so. They had four grown children and three grandchildren. Dale became ill on the day before Christmas, and in Claire's words, "when I stood at his grave on New Year's Day I felt as though my life was over." She described the shock at the sudden death of her husband, the consuming grief that followed, and the weeks and months of loneliness. She said that she cried herself to sleep most nights, "acted crazy," and often wished she could die also. Claire told how she kept the house the way her husband wanted it and made sure his clothes were ready, "as though he would come home today and need them." This went on for almost a year.

Then the housing office at the local university asked her to rent a room in her large house to foreign students. She said she was at first apprehensive about having strangers in her house, but she agreed to accept two young men from Germany. She soon became involved in a committee of community and university people who were interested in working with students from all over the world. Claire had not attended college, but she was interested in other cultures and she was an expert in human relations. She worked closely with the university office for foreign students, and the director soon recognized Claire's talents and enthusiasm. He offered her a job coordinating housing and social activities for the large contingent of students from Europe and the Middle East. Claire said she "hadn't worked outside the house for almost thirty years, and the idea scared me. But I jumped at the chance. I love it! I can't wait to get to that office to see what's going to happen next."

The loss of someone who has been a part of our life brings a grief experience that is at times overwhelming. But most people are able to reorient their lives, and in time they can return to their usual—or even new—activities.

MOST PEOPLE WHO DIE ARE OLD

It may be true that "no one ever died of old age," but the probability of death increases with advanced age.

According to the U.S. Public Health Service the five leading causes of death are (1) diseases of the heart, (2) cancer, (3) stroke, (4) accidents, and (5) influenza and pneumonia. The median age of individuals dying from heart disease and stroke is 75.7, from cancer 68.2, and from influenza and pneumonia 74.2. The median age of people dying from accidents is 39.9.

Of course people die at all ages, but over 70 percent of the people who die in any given year in this society are 70 or older. Thus, with luck, most middle-aged people have several years left to make the most of life.

Chapter 8

The Impact of Change

Today we are viewing the impact of the third
tidal wave of change in history . . . the third wave
is creating a new civilization in our midst with
its own jobs, lifestyles, sexual attitudes, concepts
of life, and political mindsets.

Alvin Toffler

In ancient Greece the average life expectancy was approximately 20 years. Of course some people lived to be 50 but they were viewed as elderly and constituted less than 1 percent of the population. During the Middle Ages a person could expect to live for 30 years if she or he could escape the plague, war, or starvation. Two hundred years later the brave, and sometimes desperate, adventurers who landed on the shores of America could reasonably expect to celebrate their thirty-seventh birthday. Several lived to see 60, and a few hearty souls lived out their alloted threescore and ten years. But the increase from 20 to 31 years took a thousand winters, and the jump from a life expectancy of 31 to 37 took 600 more years.

Our grandparents or great-grandparents, born around 1900, could expect to live fifty years: today we can expect to live seventy-five or more years, an increase of twenty-five years in less than a century! The change is phenomenal—the result of numerous factors, including scientific advances that enable us to prevent and control disease and also changes in the way we live.

Middle-aged people, unlike our ancestors, are still active,

healthy, developing, and changing. Moreover, if projections about the increasing life span are correct, a 50 year old, healthy in 1984, can expect to live thirty-two more years. This is sufficient reason for a discussion of change in a book about midlife.

An "Age of Change"

During this century we have witnessed the emergence of a new civilization. Change, on a scale previously unknown, has almost obliterated the civilization that many of us were born into. Toffler wrote that the overwhelming majority of all the materials we now use in daily life were developed in this century. Anyone who is middle aged today cannot help but be impressed by the changes that have taken place in the short span of his or her own life. Older persons are even more aware of shifts in the world around us and the effects of change on the way we live. What do older people think about the world today? One 79-year-old woman, still physically spry and mentally alert, responded to this question as follows:

Well, some of it, I think, is ridiculous. Like the crime and the drugs; I think that is awful and it ought to be stopped. God will step in one day I tell you, and He will put a stop to it.

But some of it I like, and some things are a whole lot better. People have it easier now, particularly the farmers and them that has to work hard. Why, when I was growing up we had no electricity, no way to keep our food for very long, and it was hard on the women, and men too.

I well remember when we got lights, then later a refrigerator. That was a big day! And cars! I saw a car when I was a child, but I never was in one until I was a grown woman. No cars, and no roads. Roosevelt built the roads for people you know, and you could go places. I never got to go anyplace hardly until I was a married woman, then we could go on a bus.

But the biggest thing is the doctoring. Yes sir, they can cure people's sickness now. In my day it was bad. They didn't have the medicines we have now. Oh, they tried, but they couldn't help much. I know of babies that died of whooping cough, and some got the measles and died too. And my boy Martin almost died twice—once from the fever and once when he got poisoned. But now the doctors know about all those things and they can help people. Yes sir, that's a good thing I believe. . . .

Some people resist change and long for the good old days; others accept it and may welcome it. My hope is that this section will help the reader understand it.

Values Reorientation

All adults must learn to cope with change—both internal and external. In fact, one measure of adaptation is our ability to manage change in the world we live in and change in ourselves. For many middle-aged men and women, normal change is magnified because this is an era in life when several new events and transitions occur. Re-evaluation of life goals, biological change, and children growing up are some examples of critical midlife events.

Cultural change also alters people's lives and influences all aspects of living: economic standards, mobility, freedom of choice, and love and work. Some of the most visible cultural changes of the past two decades have occurred in rules of personal conduct. Social values have changed markedly, traditional rules have been discarded, and new rules have been adopted. The new rules are more tolerant, encourage more individual freedom, and place more emphasis on personal enjoyment. The new rules for personal conduct, including greater sexual freedom, create some anxiety and require complex adaptive strategies for many adults, and they raise some unique questions for the middle aged. People in the 40 to 60 age group in the 1980s have witnessed greater social change in a few years than other generations experienced in a lifetime. The changes have often been abrupt and intense; old values are obliterated overnight, and new ways of living in a complex world must be learned in a short time.

In a changing social climate, anxiety and ambivalence are exacerbated, since social values, roles, and standards are also in a state of change. One reaches middle age and discovers that the rules and values are almost the reverse of what one learned as a child or adolescent. Discrepancies between one's own beliefs and experiences and the values and activities of the younger generation increase uncertainty and anxiety about our own values and beliefs. Middle-aged adults find themselves re-evaluating their own values at a time when they are also expected to provide guidelines for the next generation and when they are dealing with their own aging.

Responsibility and Power

Erikson, Havighurst, and other behavioral scientists believe that one major task of middle-aged persons is to provide help to both younger and older generations. Adolescents and young adults typically require not only economic help from their parents, but also direction and advice in major decision-making. As parents provide material assistance, they generally reserve the right to exercise some control over the actions of their offspring. In this process, parents have numerous opportunities to demonstrate their values, their views about the world, and their style of relating to other people.

Theoretically, elderly retired people live on what they earned earlier in life—Social Security, savings, and private retirement plans. But in fact, many retirees cannot take care of themselves, and money for their support must come from other sources. By and large, money spent through Social Security comes from taxes of currently employed persons—from young persons and the middle aged.

It is not only the middle-aged person's own children or parents who receive help. Middle-aged people are actively involved in helping numerous other persons develop their full potential as human beings. Middle-aged workers serve as mentors for young workers; teachers serve as mentors for their students, and established professionals try to help young colleagues get started.

The process of helping others is continuous; it goes on for at least as long as one is active in some cases for as long as we live. And the helping has a significant values impact, not only on the person helped, but on the total society.

Joanne Stevenson has written that the major responsibility for the continued survival and enhancement of the nation falls upon the middle aged. People between 40 and 60 are given the highest positions in the nation. The middle aged are the movers and shakers in business and industry, government, education, and the arts and letters. They control the economy, write the laws, and make the major decisions for all age groups. Occasionally we find congressmen or mayors who are younger than 40, but most of the influential government posts are held by people over 40. Most men who have served as president of the United States were elected when they were over 50. The majority of the boards of directors of the twenty largest corporations in this country are 40 or above, and most college and university presidents will never again see 40 (though few are over 65).

People in the 40 to 60 age group have the responsibility for dealing with the problems of a changing society and for making decisions about rapid technological advances. Value orientation is a critical issue here. A brief explanation may help to clarify this point.

Few people would argue that an automobile provides better transportation than a horse. Likewise, a rifle is better for bear hunting than a club. But some people will reason that horses do not seriously pollute the air we breathe and that wars fought with clubs do not wipe out the population of an entire village.

It is a question of values. We pay a high price for change—for technological progress. Was the discovery of atomic energy a boon to mankind or a colossal misfortune? If we continue to pollute the air do we risk ecological disaster? What are our choices? Dirty air and little unemployment, or blue skies, clear lakes, and bread lines? Again, these questions are value laden as well as complex. Our society has assigned primary responsibility for dealing with these and other critical issues to the middle aged.

Viewed in this light, the influence and the responsibility of the middle aged in this society are mind-boggling. If all people in the 40 to 60 age range went on vacation for a year, the world would go into a state of shock.

When they deal with public institutions or seek answers to their questions, Americans are fond of asking, "Who's in charge here?" There is little reason to ask. When you take the elevator to the eighteenth floor where the corporate offices are located and observe the splendor, the expensive furnishings, and the grey hair, you know who makes the decisions. When you stand in the hallway of the U.S. Senate Office Building or sit in the gallery in any state house of representatives, you need no political scientist or sociologist to tell you who has the power. Everyone knows who is in charge.

Chapter 9

Midlife Identity

If I had only . . .
forgotten future greatness
and looked at the green things and the buildings
and reached out to those around me
and smelled the air
and ignored the forms and the self-styled obligations
and heard the rain on the roof
and put my arms around my wife
. . . and it's not too late

Hugh Prather

The human species has existed on this planet for more than three million years. Until a few thousand years ago man led a precarious life in small societies that managed to exist by hunting and gathering food. Many people did not reach age 20, and chances for surviving until 40 were very small. Long before children were grown, their parents' lives had ended. Middle age—life after 40—has been a significant period in human life for only a moment in the history of mankind.

Modern society has not created middle age or old age—we have probably had the potential to live to be 80 since those days when our ancestors roamed the highlands of Eurasia or camped in the shadows of Kilimanjaro two million years ago. But primitive people died young because of the ravages of disease, accidents, warfare, and inadequate food supply. Modern society has remedied many of those problems, and we are now able to live out most of our life span, not just part of it.

Over the past 100 years, infant mortality has been dramatically reduced, we have conquered several fatal diseases, and we have the means to provide adequate food and housing for the world's people. And we are able to keep people healthy and active until they are 75 or 80. The result of these achievements is that a significant percentage of our population—more than 30 percent—is over 40. The problem of providing services and facilities to a growing population is continuous. But a new and perhaps more complex problem has arisen in the past few decades: how to provide conditions for a satisfying and productive life after 40. We know how to provide for man's physical or material needs; we are only beginning to understand psychological man. As we make our way across the life span we often find ourselves in uncharted waters. We have only limited experience in making the transition from one stage to another, and we may discover that society provides few directions for that journey. We are often anxious, wondering if we will reach 40 in darkness and fall off the edge.

As we traverse the life cycle we seek material goods less, and we begin looking for something more intangible and elusive. We are on the long journey that has occupied much of our life; the search for a personal self. The questions "Who am I?" and "Where am I going?" are not answered in adolescence or young adulthood. They are only temporarily filed away while we deal with other tasks and duties. But the uncertainty persists, and sooner or later we must again grapple with the question of a personal identity.

At about age 40, men and women begin a critical reassessment of the meaning and validity of their lives. We are no longer young, but we are not old: we are in fact in "our prime," and much of our life lies ahead. It is therefore quite proper that we take stock of where we are and make some plans for the remainder of the journey.

Several writers have noted that in middle age for the first time we can begin to comprehend the life cycle. It is the first time that we have the facts and the experience to understand all the options and possibilities for leading a full, satisfying life. For the first time, middle-aged men and women have the freedom and the independence to make personal decisions and to plan for the future.

It is unfortunate that many popular books and articles on midlife tend to leave the impression that this is a period of panic and depression. Evidence for this position is often based on limited data, tainted by questionable research methods. Some adults at middle age do experience a malaise, often brought on by culturally programmed demands and early experiences. But most adults in the 40 to 60 age range have developed effective coping strategies, and they are familiar with both the pleasures and the pitfalls of life. After all, they now have several years of experience to back up their knowledge.

Neugarten suspects that we have devoted too much attention to the "midlife crisis," and she questions its validity. The stages in adult life can be viewed as normal turning points, and most people do not "get off the track" when they pass the midlife milepost. They keep going, changing, and growing: many people start new families, new jobs, and new avocations when they are 40, 50 or 60 years old. The normal turning points along life's journey may result in changes in the self-concept and identity, but whether or not they create a crisis depends on numerous factors, and not on age alone.

Big Walnut Institute sits halfway up a craggy mountain in the northeastern United States. The forest surrounding the institute is dense in places and includes pine, scrub oak, maple, and poplar. A one-lane road winds up the mountain to the hotel and several smaller buildings that house meeting rooms, two dining rooms, and a library.

Big Walnut is twenty-one miles from a medium-sized town with a small airport and four miles from the nearest village. It is a quiet, beautiful place. On clear days where there is a break between the trees you can see a lush valley extending several miles east. There is a feeling of solitude as you walk the trails that wind around the rocks and across the rugged terrain.

Three thousand people traveled this narrow road last year. They were doctors, lawyers, teachers, psychologists, business executives, and students who paid $750 to attend a five-day workshop conducted by the institute. Sensory-Awareness programs and Group Therapy workshops are designed to provide personal therapy to participants and to train professional counselors, psychologists, and other helping persons.

Michael Watts, a 41-year-old executive, is participating in a sensory awareness group. His company has given him time off and is paying all of his expenses. He had been on the institute's waiting list for almost a year. He is happy to go to Big Walnut. Michael is being groomed for a bigger job with his company.

The brochure for the institute states: ". . . programs will give participants a new sense of purpose and direction . . . heighten sensitivity, and help develop a new sense of self and of potential." In another section the institute promises to "help man get in touch with a higher self" to develop a new "relationship with the Universe."

Michael said the five days were among the most rewarding of his life. The sensory awareness group "opened my eyes," he said, and made him understand and appreciate who he was. Michael hugged several people before he left.

There are numerous institutes and countless experts in this country whose major activity is to help people "grow personally" or "discover the real self." Like most inventions, they work—sometimes. But if one cannot attend a workshop at Big Walnut or does not choose individual counseling, what else helps us discover who and what we are?

There are probably some middle-aged adults who feel that they have finished the quest for a unique identity. They have discovered who they are, where they are going, and how to get there. But few people between 40 and 60 are so content or so passive. Most midlife adults are still exploring—still engaged in numerous activities that lead to self-discovery. The 50-year-old grandmother who enrolls in an adult degree program in a nearby university is responding to an urge to expand her understanding of life—and herself. The retired jeweler who begins a new career in publishing is confident that he can be successful in a new venture. The role of self-image in the lives of these adults is clear. Their actions illustrate a desire to explore new opportunities and challenges afforded by a new situation. The existential philosophers point out that choosing new paths that call for new actions—searching beyond the bend in the river—leads to the development of the real self. Choosing new courses of action and developing new awareness of the self can at times be frightening, but it can also be rewarding. It leads to authentic being, or being real. Authentic being is a sign of healthy personality.

This real self is also the product of human interaction. Our world is filled with thousands of human interactions—both negative and positive. Over the years we receive numerous messages from other human beings about who we are and what we are. Our values, our views about the world, and most important, our views about ourself are in part derived from our interpretation of the views of others. During adolescence, when our efforts to become an independent adult were most intense, we listened carefully to the messages of our peer group. By middle age, with more experience and more wisdom, we become more discriminating, more independent and more selective in our actions. By 40 or 50 we are more free to examine the ideals that guide our conduct, more willing to follow our own conscience, and less likely to conform to the views of others. When we reach middle age, we are generally more willing to acknowledge the truth of our feelings, beliefs, and wishes. And we can freely reveal our true self to other persons with whom we have a close relationship. We become more transparent, more real, more authentic.

There are times, usually during periods of unusual stress, when some of us feel deep anxiety about who we are and what we are. Erikson speaks of *identity* and *anxiety*, and other authorities write about losing one's self or becoming alienated from the self. This feeling of anxiety may come when a person examines his or her life and concludes that it is quite imperfect, or awakens one morning with the feeling that life has become drab and routine. This may lead to an attempt to escape, to project oneself into other identities, and to assume other roles. For most people, fortunately, this dimming of a usually healthy identity is temporary. But for a few, who see their potentialities blocked and their self stifled by conditions beyond their control, serious problems may result.

The most important signs along the journey of life are positive. Vaillant, Schlossberg, Neugarten, and others all describe possibilities for continued growth through the adult years. Abraham Maslow, an internationally renowned psychologist, described the unlimited potential of the "fully human person." Maslow saw man as always in a state of *becoming*—developing, learning, and becoming what he called "self-actualized." This was the highest state we could reach, and only a few made it in middle age and beyond.

Maslow believed that only mature adults could achieve their full potential. Young people, he felt, have not had enough time or experience to develop a unique identity; they have not yet acquired a sense of their place in the world, and do not yet possess the wisdom to distinguish good from evil and truth from untruth. It takes many years, according to Maslow, to assemble a *self* that is capable of achieving *self-actualization.*

The key to becoming a self-actualized person, Maslow said, was the satisfaction of basic physical and psychological needs. Such physical needs as food, safety, shelter, and sex must first be met; then a person can deal with higher level psychological needs: social, esteem, achievement, and recognition. The person who learns how to meet these needs as they arise and in a healthy manner has a good opportunity to achieve maximum development, or self-actualization.

In Maslow's view, self-actualized people exhibit the following characteristics:

1. A more adequate perception of reality and more comfortable relations with reality than found in average people.

2. A high degree of acceptance of themselves and others and of the realities of human nature.

3. Spontaneity, in thinking and in emotions.

4. Problem centeredness. Maslow's people were not problems to themselves; that is, they were not burdened by emotional maladies. Thus, they could devote their energies to a task, duty, or goal.

5. A need for privacy.

6. A high degree of autonomy.

7. A freshness of appreciation.

8. Perceptiveness. Maslow's subjects could detect the phony, the fake, and the dishonest. They preferred to deal with such matters head-on rather than retreat or deal with illusions.

9. Frequent mystic experiences. This characteristic refers to good feelings, or feelings of harmony with the self and others.

10. Close relationships with a few friends or loved ones. Self-actualized people, according to Maslow, are not necessarily popular, but tend to have close loving relationships with one or two other people.

11. Identification with mankind as a whole; concern not only for close friends, but with the situation of all mankind.

12. A strong ethical sense. Their behavior is not always conventional, but is motivated by a strong sense of what is ethically right.

13. Creativeness.

14. Sense of humor.

15. Resistance to enculturation. The self-actualized people in Maslow's study resisted attempts at brainwashing and imprinting by their culture. They tended to adopt critical attitudes toward rules, inconsistencies, and unfair practices.

Life does not run so smoothly that we satisfy all of our needs and achieve all of our goals. Maslow pointed out that most people who are normal are partially satisfied in their basic needs and partially unsatisfied at the same time. He notes also that new needs often appear as we make the journey through life.

Middle adulthood, like other stages of life, is a dynamic and changing time for all people. Chronological age may be less important in charting this part of life's journey than our quest for a unique self. This is a period when we release ourselves from the constraints of earlier decisions and begin planning the second half of life. We must learn to ignore the myth that the journey after 40 is all uphill; a most delightful trip lies ahead.

Some Simple Suggestions

Ask yourself: Who do I think I am? Is this *self* congruent with the person I want to be? If the answer to the second is *yes,* go no further. But if the answer is *no* ask yourself: How can I become the person I wish to be?

If you do not like things as they are—if you are dissatisfied with the person you are—then develop a plan for change, and work toward becoming the person you wish to be.

ERIKSON'S STAGES OF DEVELOPMENT

Erik Erikson, noted psychoanalyst, was one of the first persons to describe the psychological tasks of adulthood. He believed that each of us travels through the several stages of life attempting to master the various age-related tasks that lead us to peace and contentment in our later years.

Middle age brings with it what Erikson describes as either *generativity* or *self-absorption* and *stagnation*. By generativity, Erikson meant that the person is concerned with others and not with just his or her own needs. The person interested in society and in the quality of the world in which future generations will live. Those who fail to develop a sense of generativity may fall into a state of self-absorption, of being concerned primarily with their own needs and comforts. They may become one-sided, dwelling upon health, money, or other personal interests.

One who achieves the task of *generativity* now develops a sense of *integrity*. This sense, in Erikson's view, means the acceptance of one's life cycle: life has been lived and there is no turning back, no starting over. There is increased awareness of the self and the world, a mellowing and a warming up. In this state fear and anxiety are minimized, and death loses its sting.

Chapter 10

Coping with the Seasons of Life

The Master said, at 15 I set my heart to learning.
At 30 I planted my feet firmly on the ground.
At 40 I no longer suffered from perplexities.
At 50 I knew what were the biddings of heaven.
At 60 I heard them with docile ear.
At 70 I could follow the dictates of my own heart. . . .

Confucius

There are three quite different views about the importance of age in adult lives. There is the view that we change dramatically as we grow older. This position implies that the changes are irreversible and decremental. Another position is that we change as we reach 40 or 50, but that we are able to compensate for the biological and emotional changes of normal aging. Our attitudes about ourselves are quite important in this view. We are "as old as we feel," and we may "live to be a hundred." The third view recognizes biological change over time, but holds that we reach maturity in our late twenties or early thirties and that our behavior remains relatively stable until death.

Which view is right?

Some popular views about changes over the life span are questionable and others are inaccurate. Many of these issues have been discussed in the previous chapters; here I will make some summary statements and suggest what all of this means for middle-aged people in this century.

Most of our research on adult lives reveals some biological changes as we age, but few biological capabilities are seriously altered in middle age. Visual changes may occur after 40, but most of these are easily compensated for by corrective lenses. Some auditory loss occurs in a few people in the middle or late thirties, but the losses are generally in pitch discrimination and do not ordinarily require treatment until much later in life.

There are important cardiovascular changes in middle age. A decrease in efficient blood flow and a decline in cardiac output is experienced by a significant percentage of people over 35. And cardiovascular disease is more prevalent in people over 40. However, the percentage of persons with cardiac disorders is declining steadily, and prompt treatment of early symptoms promises further improvement. Joe D. Goldstrich, a cardiologist and past officer of the American Heart Association, states in *The Best Chance Diet* that atherosclerosis can possibly be reversed in mid-life by a combination of healthy diet (low fat, low cholesterol, low salt, low sugar), exercise, positive thinking and stress reduction. And he believes that this disease can be prevented in most people if such a regimen is adopted when young. It is our average, "normal" American diet and lifestyle that in large part causes so many average, "normal" American males (and increasingly, females) to have heart attacks, he says. Recent research seems to be leading toward the same conclusion about many types of cancer: that a healthy lifestyle, especially diet, can slow or prevent it.

Most middle-aged people know that one of the signs of biological change is in physical strength and endurance. Fifty year olds generally cannot run as far or as fast as 20 year olds (though some can), and few have a need or desire to. It appears also that there is some decline in energy level after 40, though some of this drop may be the consequence of adopting a less active lifestyle. Some of these changes are also reversible by a change in habits including diet and physical fitness programs.

Intellectually how do we change in middle age? A simple answer is: probably not much. Some earlier, and seriously flawed, research reported that after 35 we begin to experience problems with recall, learning, and problem solving. Recent research by Schaie and others has debunked this myth. Few significant changes occur in the intellect during midlife. People can and do go on learning into their seventh and eighth decade. In fact, middle-aged men and women, more than ever before, have demonstrated their interest in further learning. They are returning to school in record numbers. Mature men and women make up a significant part of the college population. This phenomenon was dubbed the "graying of the college campus" by one writer. In 1981, according to Lorraine Dorfman, there were 1.5 million adults over 35 enrolled in institutions of higher learning: 65 percent of these were women.

Over the past decade psychological changes in midlife have been discussed in detail, often in negative terms. Some of these popular views leave the impression that adult transformations are generally difficult, often traumatic, and alter most of our lives in dramatic ways. Some statements go so far as to suggest that we can all expect a midlife "crisis" and that this crisis is synonymous with pathology. It is time to bury that myth. Most middle-aged adults are not even aware that they are prone to a psychological crisis, and only a few experience one.

What are the identifiable psychological changes in midlife?

Most middle-aged people view themselves as more competent than in earlier years, both in occupational endeavors and in social interaction. By 40 or 50 most people have worked diligently on acquiring the knowledge and skill necessary to perform various adult roles, and they see themselves functioning more effectively and more independently. Middle age, sometimes called the responsible stage of life, is a time when people integrate acquired skills with role-required behavior, becoming more competent and more secure in various aspects of life.

As noted earlier, some value reorientation occurs in midlife. Lowenthal and her colleagues found a decline in material values and an increase in personal growth values among middle-aged men and women. Some research reveals a decline in career orientation and an increased interest in leisure during the middle years. It is not that middle-aged people work less—in fact many work even more—but leisure takes on more significance during this era.

One of the myths about middle age and later life grew out of a research report on sex-role reversal beginning in middle age. Soon the idea grew that men and women became more alike as they grew older. There is no good evidence for this notion, but there are strong beliefs among a few experts that as people age they become *less* alike. But we do not become different people as a result of aging. Most people at 50 are still recognizable as the people they were at 30. With the passage of years we face varied situations, respond individually to life experiences, and become unique persons, but we do not become another person when we reach the half-century milepost.

Most of the middle-aged people I have interviewed over the past five years are not as worried about the transformation of aging as some writers suggest. Fears about limited physical capacity and declining mental ability are present, but are not a major problem for most people. And they are right, because such fears are likely to be more imaginary than real. Men and women between 40 and 60 who have children are more likely to express concern about their children than about themselves. Women are likely to worry about their children's future; men worry about money and about providing for themselves and their wives in old age.

As we enter the midlife decades several changes occur that require some new adaptive strategies. Many of the changes, however, are relatively minor, and most individuals cope with them without external intervention. Some of the changes that midlife people face are the result of their own internal re-evaluation. This psychological task becomes quite important as we try to come to terms with our lives and plan for the future.

What is the recipe for coping with midlife?

Some people argue that a happy life is found by keeping active and involved. McLeish argues that we must move creatively through all the stages of life. Though we age biologically, the mind remains active, and we must use our intellect to guide us through the journey. McLeish believes that we can start new careers, new marriages, and new lifestyles at any age; change keeps us young in heart and spirit.

Flexibility and openness are also characteristics that appear to be helpful in dealing with midlife issues. Changes are inevitable in our lives and in our environment, and though some may be unwelcome we are often required to adapt to them.

There is some good evidence that those who can deal with reality are those who adapt most easily to changes around them and to variations in their own lives. People who cope effectively are those who are in touch with what is going on—they have a firm hold on reality. They also have some awareness of what lies ahead; they try to prepare for the future and act in self-directed ways.

There are, of course, other characteristics and behavior patterns that are known to help us cope effectively with life changes. Having friends that one likes and admires is viewed by some as essential to successful adaptation. But the two words that provide the key to effective coping are *love* and *work*. Love and work are intertwined; they make civilization possible and human life worthwhile.

Work is a basic need. To function normally we need to work, just as we need air, food, sleep, and sex. We often complain about work, and we often suffer stress caused by our work. But we suffer more if we cannot work—only the unwell prefer not to work. Work is one of the major routes to self-actualization; for many it is the primary way to demonstrate their usefulness. In middle age we often complain about "all work and no play," but those who do not work find little satisfaction in leisure. When we can afford to retire we often go on working, because work fulfills our need for activity and achievement.

The Old Testament commands us to "Love thy Neighbor as Thyself," and the world would probably be a more secure place if we followed this advice. But the reference here is not to love for a neighbor that is based on this order, but to the voluntary, spontaneous adult love that includes caring, sharing, commitment, loyalty, reciprocity, and sexual expression. Love does not mean being trapped in marriage and domesticity: it is a voluntary relationship, and regardless of religious or legal sanctions, it includes attachment and intimacy.

Intimate relationships allow us to know who we are; we find our identity in the person or persons we love and who love us. Love provides meaning for our life and fulfills many of our basic needs.

People can live without either love or work, but they live better, and longer, with both.

LIVING TO BE 100

What would society be like if the average age of the population was 40 and large numbers of people reached 100 or 120? Would it make sense, for example, to buy life insurance at 30?

Biologists who study the secrets of aging suggest that significantly longer life expectancies are a definite possibility in the foreseeable future. The control of major disease, proper diet, and physical fitness are all factors that can increase our life span.

Researchers estimate that by the year 2025 America will have close to 50 million people over 65 years old. Most of these people will be active and healthy. Moreover, it appears that life may improve with age. One 60-year-old attorney remarked: "Life gets better and better. You want to know why? You are free; you are not tied to mortgage payments and feeding the children. You have time and endless opportunities opening before you."

Selected References

Archbold, Patricia. "Impact of Parent-Caring on Women," *Family Relations*, 1983, 32, 39–45.

Aries, Philippe. "Mentality as History," *The Wilson Quarterly*, Winter 1981, 103–113.

Aslanian, C. B., and Brickell, H. M. *Americans in Transition: Life Changes and Reasons for Adult Learning*, Princeton, N. J.: College Entrance Examination Board, 1980.

Bardwick, Judith. "Middle Age and a Sense of the Future," *Merrill Palmer Quarterly*, 24:3 November 1978.

Bayley, N., and Oden, M. H. "The Maintenance of Intellectual Ability in Gifted Adults," *Journal of Gerontology*, 10:1, 91–97, 1955.

Becker Ernest. *The Denial of Death*, New York: MacMillan 1973.

Berger, Evelyn. *Triangle: The Betrayed Wife*, Chicago: Nelson-Hall, 1972.

Brim, Orville. "Selected Theories of Male Mid-Life Crisis," Division 17 American Psychological Association, New Orleans APA Convention, 1974.

Bureau of the Census, "Statistical Abstract of the United States," Washington, D.C., 1980.

Chiriboga, David A. "Adaptation to Marital Separation in Later and Earlier Life," *Journal of Gerontology*, 1982, 37, 109–114.

Costa, Paul, and McCrae, Robert. "Still Stable After All These Years: Personality As a Key to Some Issues in Adulthood and Old Age," in Baltes, P. and Brim, O. (Eds.) *Life-Span Development and Behavior*, Vol. 3, 1980, New York: Academic Press.

Crystal, J. C., and Bolles, R. N. *Where Do I Go From Here With My Life*, New York: Seabury Press, 1974.

Dempsey, David. *The Way We Die*, New York: McGraw Hill, 1975.

Dorfman, Lorraine T. "Reaction of Housewives to the Retirement of Their Husbands," *Family Relations*, 31, April, 1982, 195–200.

Erikson, Erik. *Childhood and Society* (2nd Edition), New York: W. W. Norton Co., 1963.

Erikson, Erik. *Identity and the Life Cycle,* New York: International University Press, 1959.

Foxley, Cecilia H. *Nonsexist Counseling,* Dubuque: Kendall/Hunt, 1979.

Freud, S. *The Psychopathology of Everyday Life,* London: The Hogarte Press (1901), 1960.

Friedman, M., and Rosenmann, R. H. *Type A Behavior and Your Heart,* New York: Knopf, 1974.

Gale, Raymond. *Who Are You?,* Englewood Cliffs, New Jersey: Prentice Hall, 1974.

Golan, Naomi. *Passing Through Transitions,* New York: The Free Press, 1981.

Goldberg, Herb. *The Hazards of Being Male,* New York: New American Library, 1976.

Goldstrich, Joe D., M.D. *The Best Chance Diet,* Atlanta, GA: Humanics Ltd., 1982.

Gould, Roger L. *Transformations: Growth and Change in Adult Life,* New York: Simon and Schuster, 1978.

Hale, Nathan. "Freud's Reflections on Love and Work," in Smelser and Erikson (Eds.), *Themes of Love and Work in Adulthood,* Cambridge, MA: Harvard University Press, 1980.

Havighurst, Robert. "Life-Span Developmental Psychology and Education," *Educational Researcher,* November 1980, 3–8.

Holmes, J., and Rahe, S. "A Social Adjustment Scale," *Journal of Psychosomatic Research,* 1967, *11*, 213–218.

Horn, J. L., and Cattell, R. B. "Refinement and Test of the Theory of Fluid and Crystallized Intelligence," *Journal of Educational Psychology,* 57, 253–270, 1966.

Horn, James. "Human Ability Systems," in Baltes, P. B. (Ed.), *Life-Span Development and Behavior,* Volume 1, New York: Academic Press, 1978.

Hultsch, David F., and Plemons, J. K. "Life Events and Life Span Development," in Baltes, P. and Brim, O. (Eds.) *Life Span Development and Behavior,* Vol. 2, New York: Academic Press, 1979.

Jacques, Elliott. "Death and the Midlife Crisis," *International Journal of Psycho-Analysis,* October 1965, 502–514.

Johnson, Elizabeth, and Spence, Donald. "Adult Children and Their Aging Parents," *Family Relations, 31,* 2, 115–122, January, 1982.

Jourard, S. M. "Marriage Is for Life," *Journal of Marriage and Family Counseling,* 1:3, 1975, 199–208.

Jung, C. C. *The Undiscovered Self,* New York: New American Library, 1958.

Katchadourian, H. A. "Medical Perspectives on Adulthood," in Erikson (Ed.) *Adulthood*, New York: W. W. Norton, 1978.

Kaye, Harvey. *Male Survival: Masculinity without Myth*, New York: Grosset and Dunlap, 1974.

Kinsey, Alfred; Pomeroy, W. B., and Martin, C. *Sexual Behavior in the Human Male*, Philadelphia: W. B. Saunders, 1948.

Kinsey, Alfred; Pomeroy, W. B., and Martin, C. *Sexual Behavior in the Human Female*, Philadelphia: W. B. Saunders, 1953.

Kirk, C. F., and Dorfman, L. T. "Satisfaction and Role Strain among Middle Age and Older Reentry Women Students," *Educational Gerontology, 9,* 15–29, 1983.

Knowles, Malcolm. *The Adult Learner, A Neglected Species* (2nd Ed.), Houston: Gulf Publishing Co., 1978.

Knox, Alan B. *Adult Development and Learning*, San Francisco: Jossey-Bass, 1978.

Kubler-Ross, Elizabeth. *On Death and Dying*, New York: Macmillan, 1969.

Lawrence, M. W. "A Developmental Look at the Usefulness of List Categorization as an Aid to Free Recall," *Canadian Journal of Psychology*, 1967, *21*, 153–165.

Lear, M. W. "Is There a Male Menopause?" *New York Times Magazine*, January 28, 1973.

Lehman, H. C. *Age and Achievement*, Princeton, N. J.: Princeton University Press, 1953.

Lenninger, George. "Sources of Marital Dissatisfaction Among Applicants for Divorce," *Journal of Orthopsychiatry*, 1966, *36*, 803–807.

Levinson, Daniel, et al. *The Seasons of a Man's Life*, New York: Ballantine Books, 1978.

Lidz, Theodore. *The Person*, New York: Basic Books, 1977.

Lindermann, Erich. "Symptomatology and Management of Acute Grief," *American Journal of Psychiatry, 101,* 2, Sept. 1944, 141–148.

Livson, F. B. "Marriage and Other Crises of Middle Age," in Troll and Israel, 1978.

Lowenthal, Marjorie; Thurnher, Majda; and Chiriboga, David. *Four Stages of Life*, San Francisco: Jossey-Bass, 1976.

McGill, M. E. *The 40 to 60 Year Old Male*, New York: Simon and Schuster, 1980.

McLeish, John A. B. *The Challenge of Aging*, Vancouver: Douglas and McIntyre, 1983.

McLeish, John A. B. *The Ulyssean Adult*, New York: McGraw Hill, 1975.

Malone, Dumas. "Jefferson and His Time," A review of Malone's work by Walter Clemons, in *Newsweek*, July 27, 1981.

Maslow, Abraham. *Motivation and Personality* (2nd edition), New York: Harper and Row, 1970.

Masters, W. H., and Johnson, V. E. *Human Sexual Response,* Boston: Little Brown, 1966.

Mayer, Nancy. *The Male Mid-Life Crisis.* New York: New American Library, 1978.

Morris, Desmond. *Intimate Behavior,* New York: Random House, 1971.

Neugarten, Bernice, L. "A New Look at Menopause," in *Psychology Today,* 1967, reprinted in Allman and Jaffee (Eds.), *Readings in Adult Psychology,* New York: Harper and Row, 1977.

Neugarten, Bernice L. "Must Everything Be a Midlife Crisis?" *Prime Time,* February, 1980.

O'Neill, Nena, and O'Neill, George. *Shifting Gears,* New York: Avon Books, 1974.

Parkes, C. M. "Psychosocial Transitions: A field study in Social Science and Medicine," Volume 5, London: Pergamon Press, 1971.

Pfeiffer, Eric, et al. "Sexual Behavior in Aged Men and Women," *Archives of General Psychiatry,* 1968, *19*, 755–758.

Reedy, M. N.; Birren, J. E.; and Schaie, K. W. "Age and Sex Differences in Satisfying Love Relationships across the Life Span," *Human Development, 24,* 52–66, 1981.

Rhodes, S. L. "A Developmental Approach to the Life Cycle of the Family," *Social Casework,* 1977, *5,* 301–311.

Rollins, B. C., and Feldman, H. "Marital Satisfaction Over the Life Cycle," *Journal of Marriage and the Family,* 1970, *32,* 20–28.

Rubin, Lillian. *Women of a Certain Age,* New York: Harper, 1979.

Schaie, K. Warner, "The Primary Mental Abilities in Adulthood: An Exploration in the Development of Psychometric Intelligence," in Baltes, and Brim, *Life-Span Development and Behavior,* Volume 2, New York: Academic Press, 1979.

Schaie, K. Warner. "Psychological Changes from Midlife to Early Old Age," American Journal of Orthopsychiatry, 51(2), April 1981, 199–218.

Scher, M. "On Counseling Men," *Personnel and Guidance Journal, 57,* January 1979, 252–255.

Schlossberg, Nancy. *Counseling Adults in Transition,* New York: Springer Publishing Company, 1984.

Selmanowitz, O. J., et al. "Aging of the Skin and Its Appendages," in Finch and Hayflick (Eds.) *Handbook of Biology of Aging,* New York: Van Nostrand, 1977.

Selye, Hans. *Stress Without Distress,* New York: New American Library, 1975.

Sontag, Susan. *The Double Standard of Aging,* New York: Farrar, Strauss, and Giroux, 1976.

Stevenson, Joanne S. *Issues and Crises During Middlescence,* New York: Appleton-Century-Crofts, 1977.

Stevens-Long, Judith. *Adult Life,* Palo Alto, CA: Mayfield Publishing Company, 1979.

Strehler, B. L. "A New Age for Aging," *Natural History,* February, 1973.

Super, Donald. *The Psychology of Careers,* New York: Harper and Row, 1957.

Swider, Ann. "Love and Adulthood in American Culture," in Smelser and Erikson (Eds.), *Themes of Love and Work in Adulthood,* Cambridge, MA: Harvard University Press, 1980.

Tanis, Alan, and Sadd, Philip. "How Men and Women Define Their Roles," cited in Van Hoose, W., and Worth, M., *Adulthood in the Life Cycle,* Dubuque: Little Brown, 1982.

Terkel, Studs. *Working,* New York: Avon Books, 1972.

Thorndike, E. L., et al. *Adult Learning,* New York: Macmillan, 1928.

Toffler, Alvin. *The Third Wave,* New York: Morrow, 1980.

Troll, Lillian. *Early and Middle Adulthood,* Monterey, CA: Brooks/Cole, 1975.

Tuchman, Barbara. *A Distant Mirror,* New York: Alfred Knopf, 1978.

Vaillant, George E. *Adaptation to Life,* Boston: Little Brown, 1977.

Wagenvoord, J., and Bailey, P. *Men, A Book for Women,* New York: Avon Books, 1978.

Wechsler, D. *The Measurement of Intelligence,* Baltimore: Williams and Wilkins Company, 1958.

Williams, Paul. *Das Energi,* New York: Warner Books, 1978.

Zahn, J. C. "Differences between Adults and Youth Affecting Learning," *Adult Education,* Winter 1967, 66–77.

Zube, M. "Changing Behavior and Outlook of Aging Men and Women: Implications for Marriage in the Middle and Later Years," *Family Relations,* 1982, *31,* 147–156.

Annotated Bibliography

The reference section contains a partial list of the sources used in the preparation of this book. This list of books, articles, and research reports should prove helpful to those who wish to pursue a topic further. In addition, the annotated bibliography will give further direction to others who wish to engage in more extensive study of the topics presented. The annotated bibliography includes those publications which cover the topics in this book the most comprehensively or usefully. Several of the books contain author's notes and bibliographies which some readers may find useful.

Erikson, Erik H. *Childhood and Society*, N.Y.: W.W. Norton, 2nd. Edition, 1963.

Erikson is often credited with being the founder of Adult Psychology. Certainly, he was among the first to describe, in nonmedical language, the process of becoming an adult and the meaning of adulthood. He is interested in the "healthy personality," and in his chapter on "Eight Ages of Man" Erikson describes human development in a variety of cultural and social settings. *Childhood and Society* is relevant to all aspects of our lives and it will be of interest to the general reader as well as the mental health professional.

Gale, Raymond F. *Who are You? the Psychology of Being Yourself,* Englewood Cliffs, N.J: Prentice-Hall, 1974.

This is a wise, humanistic book that helps us understand ourselves. Gale writes: "The most magnificent thing (a person) can create is the self." Gale explains how each of us can realize the full potential of his or her own humanity. To affirm our humanity we must love, be loved, and feel accepted in society. We must also participate in life if we hope to achieve authentic identity.

Golan, Naomi. *Passing Through Transitions,* N.Y.: The Free Press, 1981.

Golan's marvelous book describes the major events and transitions that shape adult life. She describes how normal people face and adjust to normal changes and transitions. Significant transitions of midlife, in Golan's view, include parenthood, geographic moves, career changes, separation, divorce and re-marriage, retirement, and facing death. The author draws upon her own experiences to provide case examples illustrating each of the major transitions. Research on adult life is also carefully analyzed and presented. Golan is primarily concerned with normal men and women; she believes that most life events can be successfully met and managed.

Gould, Roger L. *Transformations: Growth and Change in Adult Life,* N.Y.: Simon and Shuster, 1978.

This book deals with the periods of life from adolescence through middle age. Gould describes predictable changes over the life span, explains why the changes are predictable, and how to cope with them. The author maintains that each stage of life presents new tasks that must be mastered and new rules that must be learned. Each step we take leads us closer to a fully creative adult life.

Halberg, Edmond C. *The Gray Itch,* N.Y.: Warner Books, 1977.

This book is described as "a frank, insightful, practical guidebook for men in midlife and for the women who want to understand them." Halberg writes: you hit middle age and realize that 1) you're not going to move up in the company, 2) your kids don't need you much anymore, 3) you aren't the only focus for your liberated wife. Halberg describes some typical reactions to these discoveries and offers some helpful suggestions for men trying to adjust to these new problems.

Levinson, Daniel J., and Associates. *The Seasons of a Man's Life,* N. Y.: Ballantine Books, 1978.

This is the report of a study of 40 middle-aged men who discovered new patterns of midlife.

In the 1960s Jacques identified the "midlife crisis" as a *normal* period beginning in the late 30s and continuing for as long as 20 years. Jacques noted that some men suffer real disturbances during this era. In their discussion of this period, Levinson and his colleagues write: "A man at midlife is suffering some loss of his youthful vitality and, often, some insult to his youthful narcissistic pride." Levinson prefers the term "transition" in naming this period, noting that for most people the change is rather mild. But when midlife changes become disruptive and create turmoil, "crisis" may be the appropriate term.

Levinson's book is one of the best for those interested in midlife development in men. He explains the specific periods of middle age and describes some of the issues faced by men during this stage of development.

Lowenthal, Marjorie F., Thurnher, Madia, and Chiriboga, David. *Four Stages of Life,* San Francisco: Jossey-Bass, 1976.

The subtitle of this scholarly book is *A Comparative Study of Men and Women Facing Transitions.* The subjects for this study were men and women at four stages of life: high school seniors, young newlyweds, middle-aged parents, and an elder group about to retire. The authors are among the most highly respected scholars in the field. They deal with a variety of issues facing adults: concept of self, life satisfaction, family, stress, and adaptation. *Four Stages of Life* is an exceptional book, probably one of the most important in the field of adult development.

Mayer, Nancy. *The Male Mid-Life Crisis,* N.Y.: New American Library, 1978.

This carefully researched book describes the psychological problems facing many men at middle age. Mayer suggests that the changes of this period can signal personal turmoil or suggest possibilities for new beginnings. This is a positive book containing numerous case examples and valuable suggestions on how to make the midlife journey successfully.

McGill, Michael E. *The 40 to 60 Year Old Male,* N.Y.: Simon and Schuster, 1980.

This book, a report on a sociological study of 250 middle-aged men, is written for a popular audience. The publisher describes the book as "a guide for men — and the women in their lives — to see them through the crisis of the male middle years." This book contains self-help chapters titled "What to Do If He Is You" and "What to Do If He Is Him," among others.
McGill concludes that the "midlife crisis" is real and persuasive. However, he argues that middle age can also be a time for making positive changes, for developing new relationships, embracing new ideas, and discovering a new self.
This book is informative, well written, and helpful for both men and women.

McLeish, John A.B. *The Challenge of Aging: Ulyssean Paths to Creative Living,* Toronto: Douglas and McIntyre, 1983.

McLeish, the Canadian educator and writer, does not agree with the view that creativity resides in the young. In his witty, interesting book he maintains that the second half of life can be just as productive and exciting as the first. While physical powers may wane after middle age, the mind and the imagination remain active, ready to expand and transform the environment. Just as Ulysses made new voyages when he was old, so too can men and women venture forth in unexpected directions after 40 or

50. McLeish offers dozens of examples of men and women who have done so.

People of all ages will find this book quite valuable, and many will agree with Dr. McLeish: it is never too late to explore the Ulyssean life.

Rubin, Lillian B. *Women of a Certain Age: The Midlife Search for Self,* N.Y.: Harper & Row, Colophon Books, 1979.

"Appearance notwithstanding, for women, at least, midlife is not a stage tied to chronological age. Rather it belongs to that point In the life cycle of the family when the children are grown and gone, or nearly so — when, perhaps for the first time in her adult life, a woman can attend to her own needs, her own desires, her own development as a separate autonomous being." This is Rubin's description of the midlife woman.

Women of a Certain Age is a report of the author's study of 160 women aged 35 to 54. It is a superb account of the questions and issues facing mature women in a changing society. Rubin, a superior writer, takes a close look at midlife women and tells their story in a clear and vivid way. Rubin believes "there is more to midlife than hot flashes and headaches."

Schlossberg, Nancy K. *Counseling Adults in Transition,* N.Y.: Springer, 1984.

This book was written primarily for counselors and other professional helpers. Many general readers, however, will find helpful information in this excellent book. Schlossberg, a leading authority on adult development, examines several transitions that adults face over the life span. She explores the various techniques for helping people deal with life transitions and explains the possibilities for increasing one's capacity for work and love. This is a useful book that contributes greatly to our understanding of adult development.

Selye, Hans. *Stress Without Distress,* N.Y.: New American Library, 1975.

In this pioneer book on stress, Selye describes stress in everyday life and offers several suggestions on how to minimize the negative effects on the human body. Some stress is bad, of course, but according to Selye, "stress is the spice of life."
This interesting book tells us when stress is a problem; how to enjoy leisure; how work, stress, and aging relate; and how to use stress as a positive force in life. This useful book should be read by all midlife people.

Stevenson, Joanne Sabol. *Issues and Crises During Middlescence*, N.Y.: Appleton-Century-Crofts, 1977.

This soft-cover book was written mainly for academics. However, it is quite readable and could be useful for general readers. Stevenson presents a positive view of middle age; she views this period of life as a time for continuing development and for pursuing a wide range of options. Stevenson presents several implications and recommendations aimed at educational institutions and the mass media as well as suggestions for midlife people who want to learn more about their own lives.

Swider, Ann. "Love and Adulthood in American Culture", in Smelser, Neil J., and Erikson, Erik H. (Eds.) *Themes of Work and Love in Adulthood*, Cambridge: Harvard University Press, 1980.

The Swider article is quoted directly in this volume and for that reason is it highlighted here. However, there are eleven other excellent articles in this book and I have used them frequently in my work on adulthood. Smelser's chapter on love and work in Anglo-American society, Pearlin's chapter on life stress among adults, and Fiske's chapter on commitment in adulthood are all scholarly and informative. This book is most valuable for anyone who wants to learn more about the two major themes of adult life— love and work.

Vaillant, George E. *Adaptation to Life*, Boston: Little Brown, 1977.

This is the story of how 95 men lived their lives over a thirty-five year period. Vaillant's remarkable book, based on a mass of data collected by several researchers, deals with long-term mental health of men who were students in an Eastern university during the period from 1939 to 1944.

Vaillant describes how people cope: he discusses how some people manage quite effectively and how others cope badly, or not at all. He states: ". . . the sons-of-bitches in this world are neither born that way nor self-willed. Sons-of-bitches ensure by their unconscious effort to adapt to what for them has proven an unreasonable world."

This provocative book is good reading for all adults.

Subject Index

– A –

Adultery, 53

Adult learning, 37 – 40
   Change over the life span, 39 – 40
   Life change, 40

Adult life, 5
   Growth and change, 5 – 8
   See also transitions, phases.

Aging, 3
   Double standard, 3
   Change, 15 – 17
   Adaptation, 17, 30, 31

Appearance, changes at midlife, 18

– B –

Becoming one's own person, 6

Biological change, 14 – 17

Blood pressure 19

Body cell changes, 17

– C –

Cardiac function, 17

Career development, 52 – 54

Career adjustments in midlife, 54, 55
   men, 55; women, 56

Career change, 58 – 61
   See also adjustments in work

Changing standards, 105, 106

Circulatory and respiratory changes, 15

College and older adults, 43

Creativity and middle-age, 41

Crystallized intelligence, 36

Cultural change, 103, 104

– D –

Death, 91
   and midlife crisis, 96, 97
   parental death, 98
   death of spouse, 99 – 100

Developmental task, 5, 42

Divorce, 62, 75
   divorce rates, 75
   and middle age, 75 – 77

Dreams, 11

Author and Proper Name Index

About the Author

William H. Van Hoose was born in Kentucky and received his undergraduate education from Morehead State University. After military service during the Korean War, he received an M.S. degree from Indiana University and a Ph.D. from Ohio State. He has been a teacher, counselor, psychologist, and a professor at the University of Michigan and Wayne State University.

He is the author or co-author of more than 40 articles and 11 books including recent publications on *Adult Development, Counseling*, and *Ethics in Counseling and Psychotherapy*. Van Hoose recently published *Tecumseh: An Indian Moses*, a biography of the famous Shawnee Indian.

He is a professor of Counselor Education at the University of Virginia in Charlottesville.

Other New Books From Humanics New Age

Body, Self, and Soul: Sustaining Integration
Jack Lee Rosenberg, D. D. S., Ph. D., Marjorie L. Rand, Ph. D.,
and Diane Asay, M. A.

An introduction to an exciting new therapy method developed by the author of the best-seller *Total Orgasm* and his associates. This therapy, called Integrative Body Psychotherapy, blends ideas from East and West, including Tantric and Hatha yoga; Freudian, Jungian, Reichian, and Gestalt therapies; Rolfing, and meditation. Fascinating case studies show how this comprehensive approach can result in profound, lasting changes.

The Tao of Leadership
Lao Tsu's Tao Te Ching Adapted for a New Age
John Heider

This adaptation of one of China's best-loved books of wisdom will be valuable to anyone in a leadership position, whether within the family or group, the church or a school, business or the military, politics or government. Anyone who is concerned with more effective decision-making and leadership or who seeks a new understanding of the nature of things will find inspiration in *The Tao of Leadership*. "This is a particularly readable and accessible version of a great but difficult work." — *Publishers Weekly*

Body Conditioning: A Thinking Person's Guide
to Aerobic Fitness
Kenneth France, Ph. D.

Heart attacks killed author/runner Jim Fixx and cut short the career of tennis player Arthur Ashe. Many exercisers are running a similar risk. *Body Conditioning* shows how to evaluate any kind of workout and how most aerobic exercisers can decrease their risk of heart attack. Improved performance and enhanced enjoyment in exercising are common side effects of this method, but best of all, you'll be sure your exercise is *totally* beneficial by checking first with *Body Conditioning*.

These books and other Humanics New Age publications are available from booksellers or from Humanics New Age, P. O. Box 7447, Atlanta, Georgia 30309, (404) 874-2176. Collect calls for credit card orders are welcome. Visa and MasterCard accepted.